God's Love

God's Love

Sandra (Lott) Smith

Your New Life Ministries LLC

Contents

This book is dedicated to all who are faithfully doing God's will and to the memory of my son, Gerald Ray Lott II, whom God, in all His love, called home to be with Him on November 27, 2000.

It is also dedicated to my mother who went home to the Lord on December 26, 2002.

Prologue

This book is about God, the abundance of His love for all of mankind, and what God's love is really all about. God gets a bad rap too often. People tend to forget you reap what you sow. If a trial comes your way, in which the outcome may be to bring you to God, help you grow in Him, or increase your faith, God in turn will let it come to pass. Satan is behind many of them, but God gets the blame even though He uses Satan's act of closing a door to open a window.

God gave men free will. If He took free will away every time we chose to do something wrong only to prevent its consequence, He would have to take all free will away, even the good. God convicts our thoughts to do the right thing, but Satan convicts our thoughts as well and works overtime to do it. The stronger we are in Christ, the more power we have to fight Satan. It is our choice whether or not to do the right thing. When we choose to do the wrong thing, it is our choice of free will, not God's, which makes us do it. Every action has a consequence. You "reap what you sow."

As we teach our kids lessons and punish them, so does our Heavenly Father because of His tremendous love. When your trials overwhelm you, remember God's love. Simply trust in that and not the appearance of your trial. Trials are temporary. God's love is forever. You see, God, our Heavenly Father, loved us so much that He sent His One and Only Son to be the atoning sacrifice for our sins. How awesome! How many of us would give our only child to pay the price for something that someone else did? Mankind could never live up to the holiness of God. We would all wind up in hell if it were not for Jesus Christ. What an awesome show of love!

Yet, how does mankind show thanks and appreciation for this? We reject Jesus and the will of God. We want our own way. We make it offensive to even mention God or pray in public. The morality of mankind is truly heartbreaking. We all need to be on our knees begging for forgiveness instead of being ashamed to say you are a Christian!

I felt it necessary to write of God's love. To remind people of His awesome, unending, unselfish, and always faithful true love for us. It has been God and His wonderful love in my life, my heart, and my soul that inspired me and has also helped me in writing this book.

1

Creation

Creation: it is the first way in which God shows His love for us, the reason why we exist. God in all His glory created the world. Take a look outside. Have you ever just stood outside and looked at everything? As you read look at the trees, flowers, grass, the mountains and hills or the plains or farmland if you live there.

There are many different varieties of trees and flowers. Have you ever really noticed the beauty of it all, the way nature reproduces itself? Trees and flowers die during the fall and come back in the spring. That is what life is all about; rebirth and not death.

Isn't it beautiful, how the trees and flowers come back in the spring even more beautiful than before, after their leaves completely died! This goes hand in hand with babies, which are born, and our spirits as well. We are reborn when we receive Jesus Christ. (John 3:3) "I tell you the truth; no one can see the kingdom of God unless he is born again." We are even more beautiful than before when the Spirit of Christ lives within us.

The beauty of God's unfailing love shines through us and everything in the world that He created. It is truly amazing! We need to appreciate it more than we do. It wasn't always there. The intricate design of nature in itself tells of God's awesome touch of love in it all! In Isaiah, three verses stand out and describe how wonderful and powerful God is in how He created the world. Isaiah 40:12 tells of His hand in creating the earth, "Who has measured the waters in the hollow of His hand, or with the breadth of His hand marked off the heavens? Who has held the dust of the earth in a basket, or weighed the mountains on the scales and hills in a balance?" Isaiah 40:26 tells of His hand in creating the heavens, "Lift your eyes and look to the heavens: Who created all these? He who brings out the starry host one by one, and calls them each by name. Because of great power and mighty strength, not one of them is missing." To look at the beauty of the world you see the mighty hand of the Creator. Not only this, but as powerful as God is, He loves us, cares about our burdens, and wants a relationship with us. (Psalm 144:3) "O Lord, what is man that you care for him, the Son of man that you think of him?" Isaiah 40:22 helps you to see God as He is Almighty; "He sits enthroned above the circle of the earth, and its people are like grasshoppers. He stretches out the heavens like a canopy, and spreads them out like a tent to live in." Yet, He still chose us, you and me. (II Thessalonians 2:13) "But we ought always to thank God for you, brothers loved by the Lord, because from the beginning God chose you to be saved through the sanctifying work of the Spirit and through belief in the truth."

Not only did He choose us, but He already had a plan for us. (Ephesians 1:11-12) "In Him we were also chosen, having been predestined according to the plan of Him who works out everything in conformity with the purpose of His will, in order that we, who were the first to hope in Christ, might be for the praise of His glory." He is Almighty, powerful, and more loving than any of us can really comprehend! He wants to care for us as we do for our children! Praise God, for He truly is amazing! (Psalm 68:19) "Praise be to the Lord, to God our Savior, who daily bears our burdens." God created the world, but He wanted more to love.

Then, God created man. He wanted us to enjoy what He had made. Birth itself is a complete miracle! The way a baby grows from something as small as a seed into an adult! When we come to Christ, we grow like this as well; we are infants in Christ at first. As we read His Word, pray, and go through trials, we grow and mature in Christ. Our faith is strengthened as we overcome our trials and study the Bible. Through these things, we get closer to God and love Him more. We begin to realize why He created us, and His purpose and will for our lives.

Genesis 1:27 says, "So God created man in His own image, in the image of God He created him; male and female He created them." He created us to have a relationship with us, to be His family; His children. (James 1:18) "He chose to give us birth through the word of truth that we might be a kind of first fruits of all He created." As with our own children, we love them. We supply their daily needs: a home, their food, clothing, security, health needs, comfort, and protection.

We also discipline them when they do something wrong. We do this out of love to teach them to do right. So they will grow up knowing right from wrong and have self-confidence in themselves knowing that they are loved. Then they can pass this on to their own family. Our Heavenly Father disciplines us in the same way, so we will grow spiritually and pass on the love He shows us to others. Everything He does is out of His wonderful love and plan for our lives; He loves us. (Psalm 145:13) "The Lord is faithful to all His promises and loving towards all He has made." That is all of us, the world, and everything in it. Matthew 22:39 says, "Love your neighbor as yourself" because that is who God is; (I John 4:16) "God is Love." (I John 4: 19) "We love because He first loved us." He loved us when He created us to be His children. (Jeremiah 31:3) "I have loved you with an everlasting love; I have drawn you with loving-kindness."

To prove His love further, when man's sins were so numerous that we would never be able to make atonement for them, He sent His One and Only Son to be that atonement! That is love! (John 3:16) "For God so loved the world that He gave His One and Only Son, that whoever believes in Him shall not perish but have eternal life."

Furthermore, there is nothing we can do in ourselves to earn forgiveness. It is a gift. Free! This is truly amazing to me! (Ephesians 2:8-9) "For it is by grace you have been saved, through faith-- and this not from yourselves, it is a gift of God-- not by works, so that no one can boast."

All we have to do to receive this gift is believe in Jesus and receive-- ask Him into our hearts. (John 1:12) "Yet to all who received Him, to those who believe in His name, He gave the right to become children of God."

How truly easy it is to become brothers and sisters of Jesus Christ, true children of God. Some people make it harder than it really is, God wants us all to be united as one with Jesus Christ in eternity. (Mark 10:6-8) "For this reason, a man will leave his father and mother and be united to his wife, and the two will become one flesh. So they are no longer two, but one." Being united as one with our husbands is an example of the unity we will have with Jesus Christ in eternity one day. It is really simple to be a child of God. We make it hard.

God is our Heavenly Father. He is love. (Psalm 36:5) "Your love, O Lord, reaches to the heavens, your faithfulness to the skies." He is always faithful and forgiving. (Numbers 14:18) "The Lord is slow to anger, abounding in love and forgiving sin and rebellion." He loves us. He created us to be His children with Him in eternity. Why would anyone not want this? (Ephesians 1:4-6) "For He chose us in Him before the creation of the world to be holy and blameless in His sight. In love, He predestined us to be adopted as His sons through Jesus Christ, in accordance with His pleasure and will-- to the praise of His glorious grace, which He has freely given us in the One He loves."

This is true love. Man on his own cannot live up to this standard and with God's help, we can be transformed. We only need to ask (James 4:2) "You do not have, because you do not ask God." We also need to read His Word daily. This is how He helps to guide our steps once we decide to live for Christ, (Romans 12:2) "Do not conform any longer to the pattern of this world, but be transformed by the renewing of your mind." Spending time with God and His Word daily, not just on Sundays, is what renews our minds. He not only guides our steps in this, but we grow closer to Him as a result.

As long as you put your trust and love in God, He will lead you to victory! (Psalm 60:12) "With God we will gain the victory, and He will trample down our enemies."

He created us out of love. He came to bring life. He gives life to a soul that feels dead inside. (John 11:25-26) "I am the resurrection and the life. He who believes in Me will live, even though he dies; and whoever lives and believes in Me will never die. Do you believe this?" After receiving Jesus into your heart, as He was raised from the dead, so will your spirit. You will feel alive inside with a heart and soul all fresh and brand new! (John 10:10) "The thief comes to steal and kill and destroy; I have come that they may have life and have it to the full." Satan destroys your soul. He is the one who makes you feel dead inside, Jesus gives life. (Ephesians 4:14) "Wake up, O sleeper, and rise from the dead, and Christ will shine on you."

God loves us, and He does not want something that He created out of love to be hurt or destroyed. When you think of things in those terms, it really should not be that hard of a decision to make to follow Him.

2

Mercy & Compassion

God in all His love and mercy saved a wretched sinner: me. He who is holy and righteous has more compassion and mercy than anyone can comprehend. We hurt Him over and over and He still forgives, He still blesses, He still encourages us and lifts our spirits high. Can any of us do that, and as easily as He does? I know from experience just how much love and compassion He shows us. I am a sinner and my sins brought me to the saving grace of our Lord Jesus Christ. He forgave my sins. (Hebrews 8:12) "For I will forgive their wickedness and remember their sins no more."

He not only forgave me but has always been there for me. God's word says, (Psalm 139:16) "All the days ordained for me were written in Your book before one of them came to be." My youngest son's time came on November 27, 2000. If I had not been a child of God at that time, I would have gone with him. Gerald Ray was loving and sweet and always obeyed, he had a heart of gold. He was only 16 years old when he died. But God had other plans for me and He still needed me here. He had mercy and compassion on me and gave me a strength that I didn't have in me. (Psalm 34:18) "The Lord is close to the brokenhearted and saves those who are crushed in spirit." The Lord sure was there for me. I have made it day after day by His grace alone. He picks me up and encourages me. He reminded me that I had another son and a husband who desperately needed my love. God was there for me and I needed to be there for them.

The Lord has taught me a lot through the trials I have been through. He has taught me to trust Him. Your joy comes from Him. (John 15:11) "I have told you this so that My joy may be in you and that your joy may be complete."

Believing in and trusting our Lord Jesus Christ brings you peace and joy. He will keep you in all your ways and show His compassion and mercy to you. (Psalm 103:8-10) "The Lord is compassionate and gracious; slow to anger, abounding in love. He will not always accuse, nor will He harbor His anger forever; He does not treat us as our sins deserve or repay us according to our iniquities."

All through the ages the Lord has shown His mercy and compassion to those who love Him. (Psalm 103:13) "As a father has compassion on his children, so the Lord has compassion on those who fear Him." Our Heavenly Father understands how hard it is to live here on earth. (Romans 3:23) "For all have sinned and fall short of the glory of God." If you recognize this and come to Him just like the prodigal son in Luke 15:11-32, the Lord will always be happy to welcome you back. (I John 1:9) "If we confess our sins, He is faithful and just and will forgive us our sins and purify us from all unrighteousness."

There have been so many times when, as hard as I tried to do right, I would forget to let the Holy Spirit guide my thoughts and ways. I will lose my temper and fly off the handle at my husband or son and then feel God's conviction sweep over me. When this happens, if you are one of God's children, you can't help but go to Him and ask forgiveness. He always picks me right back up and encourages me. Joelle (a very good friend in the Lord) will call and quote me a verse that I really need to hear. That is how God works. He speaks to our hearts, through His Word, and through us. He uses us to be His vessels. But we have to be willing to let Him use us. God is full of mercy and He calls us to (Luke 6:36) "Be merciful just as your Father is merciful."

Our Heavenly Father is merciful even when He disciplines us. We all know that if you care about your children when they do something wrong, you will discipline them so they will learn and not do it anymore. God showed His mercy in the way He disciplined Cain. In Genesis 4:13, God made Cain a restless wanderer on earth. He banished him from the land of his father for killing his brother.

A "restless wanderer" is how we all feel when we are not abiding in our Heavenly Father, just like Cain. Cain did not understand that we love our children equally. They have different talents but are all unique in their own way. He let jealousy get the best of him. Our Heavenly Father loves us all in this way. He is faithful and loving to us all. I Corinthians 3:8-9 describes our uniqueness to God, "the man who plants and the man who waters have one purpose, and each will be rewarded according to his own labor. For we are God's fellow workers; you are God's field, God's building." Cain's heart and eyes should have been focused on his Heavenly Father. Then he would have known this and would not have been jealous of his brother. Yet, even so, God still had mercy on him.

Lamentations 3:22 says, "Because of the Lord's great love we are not consumed, for His compassion never fails." God banished him, but He also protected him from being killed by anyone. He marked Cain. So, if anyone did, they would suffer 7 times over. Cain did wrong and as a Father who loves, God had to discipline him. He also showed mercy to him by saving him from being killed. He marked him as we are all marked by the blood of Jesus when we accept Him as our Lord and Savior. We are protected and sealed until the day of redemption.

(II Corinthians 1:22) "He anointed us, set His seal of ownership on us, and put His Spirit in our hearts as a deposit, guaranteeing what is to come." This shows His love for us as well. God had this all planned out. We may have to go through trials for our growth and maturity as Christians, but God already has the course of our life planned out; we just need to entrust it to Him. (Ephesians 2:10) "For we are God's workmanship, created in Christ Jesus to do good works, which God has prepared in advance for us to do."

God knows that it is hard to live here on Earth while Satan is on the loose. Satan is the author of confusion and when you are going through a rough trial, it is hard to make the right decision when you are hurting badly. Perseverance is the key. (James 5:11) "As you know, we consider blessed those who have persevered. You have heard of Job's perseverance and have seen what the Lord finally brought about. The Lord is full of compassion and mercy." God understands how hard it is and His mercy and compassion are greater than you or I can ever imagine. (Exodus 34:6-7) "The Lord, the Lord, the compassionate and gracious God is slow to anger, abounding in love and faithfulness, maintaining love to thousands and forgiving wickedness, rebellion and sin."

When Moses went to the top of Mount Sinai to receive the Ten Commandments, the Israelites grew restless after Moses had been at the top for 40 days. They made a golden calf to worship. You would think after that awe-inspiring miracle of dividing the Red Sea for them to escape from the Egyptians, that they would have complete trust in God, but not so. God even provided manna (bread) that rained down from heaven and water from a rock at Horeb. These quick fixes, which were miracles that would be truly amazing to see, did not gain the Israelites' trust. Their lack of trust caused them to sin greatly against the Lord. But, God still forgave them. He wanted to destroy all of them. But at the intercession of Moses, God renewed His covenant with the ones who repented.

They worshiped a false god and God still forgave them. How great is His mercy! In their hearts, they did not know how to have faith in God. Their own will was still a priority, as it is with all of us before we accept our Lord Jesus Christ as our personal Lord and Savior. When we go through our trials, through the brokenness of our hearts, we learn to submit to God and accept Him and His will into our hearts and souls. God in all His mercy forgives us and the weight of our trials is lifted from our hearts. The heaviness of heart that you once felt is no longer there. There is now a peace and a lightness of heart that only comes from knowing and accepting Jesus Christ.

There are many times that the problems I face seem to overwhelm me and I get lost in depression. But once you are God's child, He never lets you stay there. He always whispers into the depths of my heart a verse or prompts me to read the Bible. A Scripture will stand out and really lift me up. God is always there for you. He always will be. (Deuteronomy 31:6) "He will never leave you nor forsake you." But, when He whispers into your heart, you must listen and obey. (James 4:8) "Come near to God and He will come near to you." God gave us free will and He is polite and very gentle. He won't make you read His Word or trust Him. But if you will listen and obey and trust the sweet whispers from God and submit to His will, He will encourage you and lift you up. He will help you go through your trials.

In growing closer to the Lord, you will find that you are much harder on yourself than the Lord is. Our Heavenly Father is more compassionate than anyone realizes. He knows what it feels like to experience weakness. The night Jesus was betrayed, in the garden of Gethsemane, He went to pray. He told the disciples that He took with Him, (Matthew 26:38-39) "My soul is overwhelmed with sorrow to the point of death. Stay here and keep watch with Me. Going a little farther, He fell with His face to the ground and prayed, 'My Father, if it is possible, may this cup be taken from Me. Yet not as I will, but as You will." After checking on the disciples twice, He prayed the same thing two more times. He was so overwhelmed with despair, that when He went back to pray the second time, He prayed more earnestly. (Luke 22:44) "And being in anguish, He prayed more earnestly, and His sweat was like drops of blood falling to the ground."

Jesus knows our weakness. At one point before my husband's salvation, I was praying and was disappointed in myself. At times it was really hard to keep going and persevere. He had a lot of anger and bitterness inside from all the times he was hurt. Because of this he had an alcohol problem and was very difficult to live with; I would get discouraged quite often. Then, I would get upset with myself for my weakness and lack of faith. I was being harder on myself than God was; God does not expect us to be perfect. He knows that won't come until we reach our heavenly home. But He does expect us to try. That is where His mercy and compassion come in; Jesus was tempted; He shared in our humanity. He understands our emotions. (Hebrews 2:14) "Since the children have flesh and blood, He too shared in their humanity so that by His death

He might destroy him who holds the power of death-- that is, the devil." His humanity helps Him to understand our weaknesses and temptations. (Hebrews 2:17-18) "For this reason, He had to be made like His brothers in every way, in order that He might become a merciful and faithful High Priest in service to God, and that He might make atonement for the sins of the people. Because He Himself suffered when He was tempted, He is able to help those who are being tempted."

As I prayed and was confessing my weakness to the Lord, He reminded me once again how merciful and understanding He is; He quietly whispered into my heart, "It is not in the momentary weaknesses that your faith is judged, it is in the getting back up." A verse in I Timothy explains the endurance that we are to strive for. (I Timothy 6:11-12) "But you, man of God, flee from all this and pursue righteousness, godliness, faith, love, endurance, and gentleness. Fight the good fight of the faith."

Listening to the Lord speak to my heart picked me up. Our God is a very good and loving God! He gave me a vision to explain His words as well. If you are in a marathon race and you fall, are you any less of a winner if you get back up and continue to go on to win the race? That helped me to understand that it is okay when we have weaknesses, as long as we go to God for comfort and get right back up.

Jesus did this with Peter when He was walking on the water. Matthew 14:22-33 tells of this; Jesus sent the disciples on ahead in a boat to the other side while He stayed to pray. About the fourth watch (about 3 to 6 AM) the wind started blowing fiercely and Jesus went out to them walking on the water. After seeing it was Jesus, Peter got out of the boat and started to walk on the water to Jesus. He only stumbled when he took his eyes off Jesus, but Jesus was there to take him by the hand and help him up.

In your trials as long as you keep your eyes on Jesus, He will keep you strong and able to endure. When you take your eyes off of Him and the victory that is already yours through Him, you will stumble. When you start looking more at the circumstances surrounding you instead of trusting God to get you through, fear will set in as it did for Peter. But thanks be to God, He is always with us. He will take your hand and help you back up. He will give you the comfort and encouragement to strengthen you and keep you going. You just need to call on Him. (James 4:2) "You do not have because you do not ask God."

God never promises immediate answers, but He does promise to be with you and to encourage and strengthen you. God never gave up on me. He continued to pursue me until I acknowledged that I was a sinner and asked Him into my heart. He didn't change His mind and come down from the cross. He followed through because He loves us. So, I could not give up on my husband. I relied on God for my strength, love, and encouragement. He always gave it to me. He will give it to you as well. Just ask. You do not have to do anything to receive God's mercy. Satan wants to make you believe that you have to earn God's mercy and forgiveness. That is not so. (Romans 11:6) "So too, at the present time there is a remnant chosen by grace. And if by grace, then it is no longer by works; if it were, grace would no longer be grace."

God has given us the grace of His forgiveness, His mercy, and compassion freely out of His abounding, endless love for us. We just have to come to Him, humble ourselves, and ask. (Romans 9:15-16) "I will have mercy on whom I have mercy, and I will have compassion on whom I have compassion.' It does not, therefore, depend on man's desire or effort, but on God's mercy." This verse shows how awesome and abundant God's love for us is, it doesn't matter what we do. God has mercy on us because of His love for us, not because of what we do. God understands that we make mistakes sometimes, but that is not going to hinder the plans He has for us. He will answer your prayers because of the mercy and compassion He has for us and the glory of His name. (Psalm 23:3) "He guides me in paths of righteousness for His name's sake."

In the book of Numbers, chapter 35, the Lord is instructing Moses to build 'Cities of Refuge.' These cities were for people to run to for safety. When someone killed someone accidentally or unintentionally, they could run to these cities for safekeeping until their trial could come up. This is an example of God's mercy. This represents Jesus Christ, who is our 'City of Refuge.' Jesus Christ is always there for us.

In the book of Exodus and Leviticus, God instructs Moses to build the Tabernacle and the Lampstand. This also represents Jesus Christ. The Lampstand was to be kept burning with oil constantly and was never to go out. This was because it symbolized God, always being there for us, day and night. It also represents the light of the Holy Spirit living within you who is always there for you to call on for your strength, love, comfort, and guidance. (John 14:16) "And I will ask the Father, and He will give you another Counselor to be with you forever." God also wants our love for Him to always be there for Him. He wants us to pray to Him and it doesn't matter when, He is always there.

God is a merciful God. Where there is true Godly sorrow and repentance, there is always mercy and forgiveness. You may have to 'reap what you sow.' There are always consequences for our actions, but you can rest assured that you are forgiven. (Psalm 32:5) "Then I acknowledged my sin to you and did not cover up my iniquity. I said, 'I will confess my transgressions to the Lord' -- and you forgave the guilt of my sin."

As God shows mercy and forgiveness to us, we are to likewise show it to our fellow man. (James 2: 12-13) "Speak and act as those who are going to be judged by the law that gives freedom, because judgment without mercy will be shown to anyone who has not been merciful. Mercy triumphs over judgment!"

3

The Bible

The Bible is another way in which God has shown His love for us. (II Timothy 3:16-17) "All scripture is God-breathed and is useful for teaching, rebuking, correcting and training in righteousness, so that the man of God may be thoroughly equipped for every good work." God created the world, man and everything in it, and the heavens above. (Genesis 1:1-2) "In the beginning, God created the heavens and the earth. Now the earth was formless and empty, darkness was over the surface of the deep, and the Spirit of God was hovering over the waters." God is Spirit and so is His Word. All He had to do was say it and it was so. (Genesis 1:3) "And God said, 'Let there be light', and there was light." God had His Word first. (John 1:1-2) "In the beginning was the Word, and the Word was with God, and the Word was God. He was with God in the beginning." The Word of God is Jesus Christ. (John 1:14) "The Word became flesh and made His dwelling among us. We have seen His glory, the glory of the One and Only, who came from the Father, full of grace and truth."

God's Word, the Bible, and Jesus Christ will sustain us through life if we trust in Him. (Hebrews 1:3) "The Son is the radiance of God's glory and the exact representation of His being, sustaining all things by His powerful Word." The world was dark before God gave it light. That is how we all live before we accept Jesus Christ. We live in darkness. The darkness of our hearts fills our spirits. Accepting Jesus as your personal Lord and Savior will bring light to your heart and spirit. (John 8:12) "I am the light of the world. Whoever follows Me will never walk in darkness, but will have the light of life."

Since the Word was first and Jesus was the Word, accepting Him will bring to life everything in the Bible that you read. What you once read before and did not understand; Jesus will bring to life in your heart. You will not only understand it, but it will have great meaning to you as well.

Before coming to Jesus, understanding the Bible is difficult to do for "unbelievers" because of Satan. He does not want you to understand it; to keep you from getting closer to God. Only God can take the blinders off. This only happens upon repentance. (II Corinthians 4:4) "The god of this age has blinded the minds of unbelievers, so they cannot see the light of the gospel, of the glory of Christ, who is the image of God." Upon repentance, God takes the blinders off and enlightens your heart with the Spirit of Christ, which brings peace and understanding to your soul. (Isaiah 6:9-10) "Be ever hearing, but never understanding; be ever seeing, but never perceiving. Make the heart of this people calloused; make their ears dull and close their eyes. Otherwise, they might see with their eyes, hear with their ears, understand with their hearts, and turn and be healed."

Our Heavenly Father created us out of love, and with Satan prowling around on the earth seeking whom he may destroy, God knew it would be hard for us. (I Corinthians 2:9) "However it is written: No eye has seen, no ear has heard, no mind has conceived what God has prepared for those who love Him." God did not create us to walk blindly. If you trust Him your path will be clear to you. (Proverbs 3:5-6) "Trust in the Lord with all your heart and lean not on your own understanding; in all your ways acknowledge Him, and He will make your paths straight."

God gave us His Word as a guide. No matter what you need, the Bible has the answer. You not only read it and write it on the pages of your mind but it is written deep within your spirit as well. (Psalm 119:9-11) "How can a young man keep his way pure? By living according to Your Word. I seek You with all my heart; do not let me stray from Your commands. I have hidden Your Word in my heart that I might not sin against You." God's Word is a guide not only for teaching you right from wrong but also guidance for every area of your life. (Psalm 119:105) "Your Word is a lamp to my feet and a light for my path."

As you read through the pages of history in the Bible, you will find that the people in Bible times went through family problems, lack of faith, marital problems, emotional problems, health problems, and problems with the people that governed over them (the people over you. today it is our political leaders and our supervisors at work or parents). You will see how God brought them through it and the message we can learn from it to help us in our walk with God and overcome the trials of life. The messages you receive from the Word of God are truly from Him. (II Peter 1:20-21) "Above all, you must understand that no prophecy of Scripture came about by the prophet's own interpretation. For prophecy never had its origin in the will of man, but men spoke from God as they were carried along by the Holy Spirit."

As you grow closer to the Lord you will find that the Word of God is Spirit, alive within your heart. (Hebrews 4:12) "For the Word of God is living and active. Sharper than any double-edged sword, it penetrates even to dividing soul and spirit, joints and marrow; it judges the thoughts and attitudes of the heart." Even in your weakest moments, if you turn to God's Word, God Himself will guide you to a passage of Scripture that will pick you up and lift your spirits. (Isaiah 40:31) "But those who hope in the Lord will renew their strength. They will soar on wings like eagles; they will run and not grow weary, they will walk and not be faint."

Our God is Sovereign and drawing near to Him in your daily walk will only bring you blessings. (Isaiah 25:8) "The Sovereign Lord will wipe away the tears from all faces." Praise be to God! He is a very loving God. (Psalm 112:1) "Blessed is the man who fears the Lord, who finds great delight in His commands." Reading the Word of God will keep you close to Him and keep Satan away; (Ephesians 4:27) "and do not give the devil a foothold." Reading His Word daily helps you to grow and mature as a Christian and bring prosperity to your heart and life. (Psalm 1:1-3) "Blessed is the man who does not walk in the counsel of the wicked or stand in the way of sinners or sit in the seat of mockers. But his delight is in the law of the Lord, and on His Law he meditates day and night. He is like a tree planted by streams of water, which yields its fruit in season and whose leaf does not wither. Whatever he does prospers."

Reading God's Word daily helps you to learn His promises and find out who God is; for God's Word is truth. (John 17:17) "Sanctify them by the truth; Your Word is truth." The promises of God are true, and the promises He makes to you through His Word will happen. (Numbers 23:19) "God is not a man, that He should lie, nor a son of man, that He should change His mind."

Our Heavenly Father is Holy, Sovereign, Powerful, and full of love and compassion. If you read His Word, and put your trust in Him, He will speak to you through His Word.

There have been many times when reading the Bible I have come across a Scripture that spoke to my heart. It just "jumped out" at me, so to speak. I knew it was from God, encouraging me. Every time that happened it always related to the trial I was going through at the time.

When God promises something, He will do it. (Isaiah 55:11) "So is My Word that goes out from My mouth: It will not return to Me empty, but will accomplish what I desire and achieve the purpose for which I sent it."

(II Samuel 22:31) "As for God, His way is perfect; the Word of the Lord is flawless." If you read His Word and etch it into your mind and heart it will bring forth blessings to your soul and spirit. It will encourage you and pick you up when you are down. (Colossians 3:16) "Let the Word of Christ dwell in you richly;" For it is the Spirit of God ministering to your spirit, through His Word. (Ephesians 6:17) "The sword of the Spirit, which is the Word of God." God's Word not only ministers to your soul, but your faith grows as well. (Romans 10:17) "Faith comes from hearing the message, and the message is heard through the word of Christ." As your faith in God grows, you grow stronger as a Christian and are more able to stand against the "fiery darts" of Satan.

(Luke 6:47-48) "I will show you what he is like who comes to Me and hears My Words and puts them into practice. He is like a man building a house, who dug down deep and laid the foundation on rock. When a flood came, the torrent struck that house but could not shake it, because it was well built." Jesus Christ is the Rock, the foundation on which our faith is built. (Isaiah 28:16) "See, I lay a stone in Zion, a tested stone, a precious cornerstone for a sure foundation; the one who trusts will never be dismayed."

God gave us His Word as a source of strength and encouragement, and to help guide our path in life. He did this out of His undying love for us. He said, (Joshua 1:5) "I will never leave you nor forsake you." His Word is just one of the ways in which God has shown His love for us and provided for us.

4

Discipline

Discipline is something that no one enjoys but is something that is needed in order to correct wrong things. Children need it as they are growing up to teach them right from wrong. Discipline helps them to grow up into mature adults who have self-confidence and can support themselves and most of all, to know that they are loved. If you see a child you do not know do something wrong, you do not correct them. There is no bond of love between you. Someone that you love and care about, you correct, because you do not want him or her to keep making wrong choices. (Proverbs 13:24) "He who spares the rod hates his son, but he who loves him is careful to discipline him." It is God's will that we correct our children, so He will not have to later. (Proverbs 23:13) "Do not withhold discipline from a child; if you punish him with the rod he will not die. Punish him with the rod and save his soul from death."

This is how it is with your Heavenly Father. Discipline is another way in which God shows His love for us. (Hebrews 12:5-7) "My son, do not make light of the Lord's discipline and do not lose heart when He rebukes you, because the Lord disciplines those He loves, and He punishes everyone He accepts as a son. Endure hardship as discipline; God is treating you as sons." He wants us to grow into mature Christians with a faith so strong it can move a mountain! Not only that, the stronger we are as

Christians, the more He can use us to help others the way He is there for us. The stronger we are in our faith, the more power we have to fight off Satan's attacks and temptations. Just as a baby has to fall several times before he can walk, so must we when we become a Christian. We learn through the corrections the Lord gives us.

We are not automatically the perfect Christian upon receiving the Lord into our hearts. We learn as we travel down the road of life and cross over the rocky mountains of our trials. The Lord's discipline is a blessing. In His discipline, you know that He loves you. (Job 5:17-18) "Blessed is the man whom God corrects; so do not despise the discipline of the Almighty. For He wounds, but He also binds up; He injures, but His hands also heal."

Discipline from the Lord is not only punishment it is also what God uses to teach us to be self-disciplined and is a source of strengthening us. For example, when you exercise, if you do it every day, it becomes a habit. It becomes something that is a part of you and what you do every day.

There have been many times when I have been caught off-guard and Satan completely overwhelmed me, and depression set in. Satan will use your weaknesses over and over. My weaknesses are my husband and my son. In some ways they are a lot alike, the way they can be so determined and strong-willed. They came to blows quite often. They both could be very hardheaded and not willing to give an inch or see the other person's point of view. Most of us can be that way when we are so determined to get our own way, myself included. After my youngest son died, it was very difficult for me to let go and let God carry the burden of dealing with them and healing the hurts that each of them had inside. Their internal pain caused them to hurt each other so often in their arguments. This overwhelmed me each time they fought. I love both of them and felt like I had to be a peacemaker instead of letting God handle it.

Sometimes you have to realize when you are talking to a brick wall, that they may be taking what you are trying to do the wrong way. I was trying to hold on to what was left of my family and that was the problem. I was trying to hold on instead of letting God hold onto all of us. He is God and He is Sovereign and can do a lot better job of putting us back together and making us "whole" children of God than I could do just trying to keep the peace.

Their fights got ugly sometimes and it hurt, knowing how much each of them hurt inside. It hurt for me and them. I would get depressed and feel lost and alone. I felt that way because I was not trusting God to handle the problem. I gave Him the problem, but every time I worried about it, I took it back. That is not trust. When you are a child of God, and as you grow as a Christian, God is harder on you than when you were an "infant in Christ." Just like when your children are capable of making an "A" in a particular subject and bring home a "D" you get angry with them and make them study harder and play less until that grade is brought back up to where you know it should be.

God is like that with us. As a baby Christian, He may give you more visible signs of knowing that He is there for you. As you grow and He sees evidence of your faith, He wants it to be there all the time, not just in the good times. Faith is faith when you can rejoice in the hard times as well. (Hebrews 11:6) "And without faith it is impossible to please God because anyone who comes to Him must believe that He exists and that He rewards those who earnestly seek Him."

This is when God knows that you really love Him and you will always be there for Him as He is for you, not just when you need His help. He gives you a knowing deep within your heart that tells you He loves you and He will answer your prayers. You must have faith. This trust in Him brings you peace even in difficult times. (Psalm 37:7-9) "Be still before the Lord and wait patiently for Him; do not fret when men succeed in their ways when they carry out their wicked schemes. Refrain from anger and turn from wrath; do not fret-- it leads only to evil. For evil men will be cut off, but those who hope in the Lord will inherit the land."

When I finally learned to trust in Him and believe that He will heal their hurts, in His time, the peace of His presence returned to my heart. He was disciplining me by standing off when I left His presence and entered into the presence of doubt.

That is why I felt so alone. You see He doesn't leave, we do. He has to answer our prayers in His time and in His way. He knows their hearts and He knows the pain in my husband and son's hearts better than I do. Just like picking fruit, if you pick it before it is ripe, it is bitter. If you wait until the harvest is ripe, then how sweet it is! That is the way it is with us. God knows the timing. After all, He is God and we are not. Everything has its season. (Ecclesiastes 3:1) "There is a time for everything and a season for every activity under heaven." This includes the trials that we go through. The longer it takes us to accept God's discipline and instructions, obeying and trusting Him, the longer it takes to get to our harvest time when our prayers are answered.

Teaching us to be self-disciplined in our daily devotions and attitude strengthens us and helps us to grow and mature as Christians. We do get angry and depressed from time to time, but it is the actions that we do or do not do that are either wrong or right. (Psalm 4:4) "In your anger do not sin."

(Proverbs 14:17) "A quick-tempered man does foolish things." Our actions speak louder than words. Our actions show the world whether or not "the light of the world" is truly in us or not. A gentle answer shows the love of Jesus within us. (Proverbs 15:1) "A gentle answer turns away wrath, but a harsh word stirs up anger." As God is merciful, understanding, and slow to anger with us, we are to be likewise with our fellow man. (James 1:19-21) "My dear brothers, take note of this: Everyone should be quick to listen, slow to speak, and slow to become angry, for man's anger does not bring about the righteous life that God desires. Therefore, get rid of all moral filth and the evil that is so prevalent and humbly accept the Word planted in you, which can save you."

As children of God, He disciplines us for our good. (I Corinthians 11:32) "When we are judged by the Lord, we are being disciplined so that we will not be condemned with the world." It is to our benefit to accept it out of the love that it is given. (Proverbs 10:17) "He who heeds discipline shows the way to life, but whoever ignores correction leads others astray."

Learning from the Lord's discipline helps us to grow, so we can move on with the plans He has for us. As we heed God's discipline and instructions, and put them into practice, we have peace as well. (Hebrews

12:10-11) "Our fathers disciplined us for a little while as they thought best, but God disciplines us for our good, that we may share in His Holiness. No discipline seems pleasant at the time, but painful. Later on, however, it produces a harvest of righteousness and peace for those who have been trained by it."

Our Heavenly Father loves us and understands how hard it is to live in the world. He knows how devious Satan is and the schemes he uses to destroy us. God has to be hard on us to strengthen us and teach us His Laws and His Word, so we are well-equipped to fight off Satan's attacks. (Psalm 94:12-15) " Blessed is the man you discipline, O Lord, the man You teach from Your Law; You grant him relief from days of trouble, till a pit is dug for the wicked. For the Lord will not reject His people; He will never forsake His inheritance. Judgment will again be founded on righteousness, and all the upright in heart will follow it."

Remember, (Romans 8:39) "Neither height nor depth nor anything else in all creation, will be able to separate us from the love of God." When we humble ourselves and learn from God's discipline, we are blessed as children of God. We are renewed in our spirits and in the plans God has for us. (Psalm 51:10-12) "Create in me a pure heart, O God, and renew a steadfast spirit within me. Do not cast me from Your presence or take Your Holy Spirit from me. Restore to me the joy of Your salvation and grant me a willing spirit, to sustain me."

As we repent, obey, and trust we gain His favor. (Psalm 30:5) "For His anger lasts only a moment, but His favor lasts a lifetime; weeping may remain for a night, but rejoicing comes in the morning."

When we stand firm and have true faith in God, we have peace in our hearts no matter what the trials of life are that come our way. (Isaiah 26:3-4) "You will keep in perfect peace him whose mind is steadfast because he trusts in You. Trust in the Lord forever, for the Lord, the Lord, is the Rock eternal."

Trust in the Lord even when you are experiencing His discipline. It will produce a harvest of righteousness. (Psalm 37:5) "Commit your way to the Lord; trust in Him and He will do this: He will make your righteousness shine like the dawn, the justice of your cause like the noon-day sun."

5

God's Faithfulness

God in His faithfulness never changes. His love is constant. He doesn't move, we do. (Hebrews 13:8) "Jesus Christ is the same yesterday and today and forever." God loves us through all our good times and bad. He loves us when we are rebelling against Him and when we submit to Him. He is very patient with us. (II Peter 3: 9) "He is patient with you, not wanting anyone to perish, but everyone to come to repentance."

God is All-Powerful, All-Knowing, and Sovereign over all things, and yet He is still gentle and patient with us. Even when we mess up and make mistakes, He still loves us. He is always there with open arms waiting for us to hear the sweet whispers of His convictions, pointing us in the right direction, and telling us what we are doing wrong. He is always there waiting for us to say "please forgive me" or to go in the direction He is trying to lead us.

God's faithfulness is another way in which He shows His love for us. Even when we are not, God is still faithful! Praise God! For He truly is wonderful! (II Timothy 2:13) "If we are faithless, He will remain faithful, for He cannot disown Himself." Without His grace, love, and faithfulness, I would not have a chance. (Romans 3:3-4) "What if some did not have faith? Will their lack of faith nullify God's faithfulness?

Not at all! Let God be true, and every man a liar. As it is written: So that you may be proved right when you speak and prevail when you judge."

Our Heavenly Father has plans for our lives. We need to submit to His will and authority. He is the One and Only Almighty Father in heaven. He is Sovereign. If He can create the world, then He is very capable of taking whatever mess that you have going on in your life and making a message out of it. (Jeremiah 29:11-14) "For I know the plans I have for you, declares the Lord, plans to prosper you and not to harm you, plans to give you hope and a future. Then you will call upon Me and come and pray to Me, and I will listen to you. You will seek Me and find Me when you seek Me with all your heart. I will be found by you, declares the Lord, and bring you back from captivity."

Once you have accepted Jesus Christ into your heart, you are then a child of God. He will always be faithful to you. You will go through many trials, but He will always be there for you. He will help you through them and provide a way out. I have found in my own experiences that whenever I did not feel the presence of the Lord in my heart, it wasn't the Lord that moved, it was me. Each time that happened He always convicted my heart. He gently showed me the way back to His path.

The trials you go through are to mold you into the Christian that God wants you to be. The things that you learn from each trial you come through will help you in the future. You will be stronger each time you make it through and you will be able to help someone else going through a similar trial. Once God has started a good work in you, trust Him to complete it. Life is a learning process. The more you are willing to learn and submit to God, the more He can use you to help someone else in need as He helps you. (Philippians 1:6) "Being confident of this, that He who began a good work in you will carry it on to completion until the day of Christ Jesus." Even if you fail along the way, God's mercy and faithfulness never end. Praise God! (Lamentations 3:22-23) "Because of the Lord's great love we are not consumed, for His compassions never fail. They are new every morning; great is Your faithfulness."

We get wrapped up so often in the trials we are going through and in the desires of our hearts, that when something happens contrary to what we thought would happen, we get bent out of shape and start to doubt. We forget that God is All-Knowing and that He loves us and He wants the best for us. (Psalm 91:1-4) "He who dwells in the shelter of the Most High will rest in the shadow of the Almighty. I will say of the Lord, 'He is my refuge and my fortress, my God, in whom I trust.' Surely, He will save you from the Fowler's snare and from the deadly pestilence. He will cover you with His feathers, and under His wings you will find refuge; His faithfulness will be your shield and rampart."

Sometimes the way God is working it out does not seem to us as if our prayers are getting answered but patience is a virtue. (Psalm 27:13-14) "I am still confident of this: I will see the goodness of the Lord in the land of the living. Wait for the Lord; be strong and take heart and wait for the Lord." When your children ask for something sweet right at dinnertime, you usually tell them to wait until after dinner, then they can have their dessert. God knows the right time to give us the answer to our prayers and in the right way. He may know a better way than the way you are thinking. His way is always better because He knows the outcome already.

In some cases, He has to work out the answers to our prayers in us little by little. (Deuteronomy 7:22) "The Lord your God will drive out those nations before you, little by little. You will not be allowed to eliminate them all at once, or the wild animals will multiply around you." As a child learns to ride a bike, he has to work his way up to a bicycle. He has to start with a tricycle, then maybe a bike with training wheels until he gets used to it. It takes time and persistence, but how joyful he is when he learns to ride! This is how the trials of life are. Through the trials you go through, your heart is changed into who God wants you to be. No matter what you are going through, God is faithful to get you through it and supply all your needs. You need to trust Him and wait on Him. (Philippians 4:19) "And my God will meet all your needs according to His glorious riches in Christ Jesus."

Do you remember the story of Joseph, son of Jacob and Rachel? His brothers were jealous of the affection Jacob had for him and sold him into slavery. Joseph was always true to God and God was faithful to him. He ended up in Egypt. God caused Pharaoh to look with favor on Joseph. Pharaoh had some dreams which, with the help of God, Joseph interpreted right. The dreams were from God. They told of seven years of plenty in the land, followed by seven years of famine. Since Joseph had interpreted the dreams correctly, Pharaoh was pleased with him and put him in charge of his palace and the whole land of Egypt.

God was working out a plan to take care of Joseph's family during the years of famine, though at first, it did not seem like it. The years of being in slavery, and even being put into prison, were probably difficult and lonely for him. He probably missed his family and at the same time was very hurt, but he trusted God. Through being in charge of the land, Joseph stored up grain during the years of plenty to make up for when the years of famine came. Through this, Joseph was reunited with his brothers and Jacob, his father. He waited on God, knowing that God had a plan, and God was faithful, and He took care of him and blessed him and his family.

Instead of his brothers killing him like they originally wanted to do, God protected him and provided an escape. God convicted the heart of his older brothers Reuben and Judah. They pleaded with the rest of his brothers not to kill him so they sold him instead. This worked out for Joseph's good and his family's as well. (II Peter 2:9) "If this is so, then the Lord knows how to rescue godly men from trials and to hold the unrighteous for the Day of Judgment while continuing their punishment." We have to remember faith pleases God. (II Corinthians 5:7) "We live by faith, not by sight." Trusting in God's love and praising Him, for the name of Judah means praise. (I Corinthians 13:8) "Love never fails."

As long as we live here on earth we will be at war with Satan. He wants to destroy everything that belongs to God. (John 10:10) "The thief comes only to steal, kill and destroy; I have come that they may have life, and have it to the full." There is a constant spiritual battle going on as long as Satan roams the earth. With God and His Word, you can be prepared. (Ephesians 6:12) "For our struggle is not against flesh and blood, but against the rulers, against the authorities, against the powers of this dark world and against the spiritual forces of evil in the heavenly realms."

As long as you are a child of God He will always be there to protect you. (Psalm 97:10) "Let those who love the Lord hate evil, for He guards the lives of His faithful ones and delivers them from the hand of the wicked." The Lord will strengthen you and protect you. You must remain faithful to Him, and love and trust Him even when it doesn't look like it.   (II Thessalonians 3:3) "But the Lord is faithful, and He will strengthen and protect you from the evil on."   It is when things look their worst, and the situation looks impossible, that God is glorified the most. (Matthew 19:26) "With man this is impossible, but with God all things are possible."

After the death of Moses, Joshua was chosen by God to lead the Israelites into the Promised Land. God promised to be with them as long as they loved, trusted, and obeyed Him. (Joshua 1:3-7) "I will give you every place where you set your foot, as I promised Moses. Your territory will extend from the desert to Lebanon, and from the great river, the Euphrates--all the Hittite country--to the Great Sea on the west. No one will be able to stand up against you all the days of your life. As I was with Moses, so I will be with you; I will never leave you nor forsake you. Be strong and courageous, because you will lead these people to inherit the land I swore to their forefathers to give them. Be careful to obey all the Law my servant Moses gave you; do not turn from it to the right or to the left, that you may be successful wherever you go." The Lord was faithful to His promises. He is always faithful.

Whenever the answers to our prayers or the plans that God has for us get delayed, we need to take a good look at ourselves. Sometimes it is not time for them to be answered. But when these plans get delayed due to a problem, the problem is with us, not God. God doesn't move, we do. He is not a man that can be tempted. (Numbers 23:19) "God is not a man, that He should lie, nor a son of man, that He should change His mind. Does He speak and then not act? Does He promise and not fulfill?"

The Israelites did enter the Promised Land, it took forty years of their forefathers wandering in the desert, but they did enter. It was due to their unbelief and complaining, their hearts were not devoted to God. As the Israelites worshiped the Lord and obeyed His Word, the Lord was faithful to His promises. (Joshua 21:43-45) "So the Lord gave Israel all the land He had sworn to give their forefathers, and they took possession of it and settled there. The Lord gave them rest on every side, just as He had sworn to their forefathers. Not one of their enemies withstood them; the Lord handed all their enemies over to them. Not one of all the Lord's good promises to the house of Israel failed; every one was fulfilled."

The Promised Land was their deliverance. As you face trials and tribulations, remember the Israelites and how God was faithful to them. Their enemies were a strong and powerful people, just as the problems that you face. There is nothing too strong or impossible for our Almighty Father in heaven. (Isaiah 54:10) "Though the mountains be shaken and the hills be removed, yet My unfailing love for you will not be shaken nor My covenant of peace be removed." (Psalm 36:5) "Your love O Lord, reaches to the heavens, Your faithfulness to the skies."

The troubles I have faced living with alcoholism and drug addiction in my family were very painful. Through that pain and suffering, I have done some things that I wish I could take back. But it brought me to the saving grace of our Lord Jesus Christ. It is very humbling to experience the love and forgiveness that He shows when you truly repent and receive Him. He gives you peace in your heart that tells you that He does love you. You know that you don't deserve it, but that is what God's love is all about. His love is about mercy, grace, and forgiveness, just because He loves us and not because we deserve it. He wants a relationship with us. God is love and that is why He is so faithful.

God has been faithful to me in everything that I have been through since the time I made Him my personal Lord and Savior. I keep making mistakes and God gently lets me know what I am doing wrong. I welcome His corrections because I only want to please Him.

I know correction is the only way of learning how to get it right. He has been there for me through the troubling times before my husband's salvation and through the death of my son. It was barely two years from the day He died when I got a phone call from my sister in Texas telling me that my mother was in the hospital. We were very close even though we lived miles apart. I always called her and visited when I could. I got the call the day after Thanksgiving. It was November 27, 2000, when my son was killed. On December 26, 2002, the Lord took my mother home. God was faithful to me then as He was with my son. He held my heart in His hand to keep it from shattering into pieces. He still holds my heart and shows me every day that He loves me. I could not have gone on if it were not for the love of God. (Psalm 145:13) "The Lord is faithful to all His promises and loving toward all He has made."

There are other examples of God's faithfulness all through the pages of history in the Bible. The Bible is not only filled with God's instructions and promises for you and your life but it is also filled with lots of wonderful stories of people. People who endured hardships, pain, and suffering, which in those times were probably more difficult to endure than what we have to endure today.

The trials and difficulties of life get rough at times but always remember that God loves you and is always faithful to you. (Psalm 117:1-2) "Praise the Lord, all you nations; extol Him, all you peoples. For great is His love toward us, and the faithfulness of the Lord endures forever."

6

∽

God Is Always With You

As a child of God traveling down life's highway, no matter what you are going through, good times or bad, your Heavenly Father is always with you. (Deuteronomy 31:8) "The Lord Himself goes before you and will be with you; He will never leave you nor forsake you. Do not be afraid; do not be discouraged." Isn't that reassuring? To know that no matter what the trial is you are going through, God has already been there ahead of you, should bring you a sense of relief and peace. It should help you to trust Him more. This is another way in which our Heavenly Father shows His love for us. Nothing happens here on earth without God's approval first. (Daniel 4:25) "The Most High is Sovereign over the kingdoms of men and gives them to anyone He wishes." (Jeremiah 27:5) "With My great power and outstretched arm I made the earth and its people and the animals that are on it, and I give it to anyone I please."

We do get discouraged when the problems we are facing seem to be overwhelming. The hurt or worry we are dealing with seems to blindside us and cause us to take our eyes off Jesus. That is when discouragement and doubt sets in. Take heart, God will not let you stay that way! He loves you and will bring you back! (Psalm 147:5) "Great is our Lord and mighty in power; His understanding has no limit."

All you have to do is ask for His help. (Deuteronomy 4:29-31) "But if from there you seek the Lord your God, you will find Him if you look for Him with all your heart and with all your soul. When you are in distress and all these things have happened to you, then in later days you will return to the Lord your God and obey Him. For the Lord your God is a merciful God; He will not abandon or destroy you or forget the covenant with your forefathers, which He confirmed to them by oath."

God lets things happen sometimes that will mold us into who He wants us to be. He also lets things happen that will lead us to salvation. God gave us free will. He wants every one of us to be unique and not robots. The trouble with that is Satan, he takes advantage of that. He will tempt you and deceive you. He is ruthless. He has to be, to have once been an angel in the presence of God and turn against Him. The light of God's love brings you peace and joy, and Satan did not want this, which I cannot understand. It just shows how evil and self-centered Satan is, and that he has no love in him. He only wants to bring harm to the ones that God loves, to get to Him. (I Peter 5:8) "Be self-controlled and alert. Your enemy the devil prowls around like a roaring lion looking for someone to devour."

So, out of God's overwhelming love for us, He will do whatever it takes to help us see the light and turn to Jesus Christ for our eternal salvation. (Job 33:29-30) "God does all these things to a man-- twice, even three times-- to turn back his soul from the pit that the Light of life may shine on him." Though things may get rough from time to time, know that God's ever-watchful eye is on you. (Psalm 121:5-8) "The Lord watches over you-- the Lord is your shade at your right hand; the sun will not harm you by day, nor the moon by night. The Lord will keep you from all harm-- He will watch over your life; the Lord will watch over you coming and going both now and forevermore." To know that God is always watching over me is very reassuring and makes me feel safe.

In everything you go through, know that God is always with you, and He will lead and guide you. (Exodus 15: 13) "In Your unfailing love you will lead the people You have redeemed. In Your strength, You will guide them to Your holy dwelling." Just as our own children have to learn from their mistakes, we need to as well. We cannot be there every minute of the day to keep our children from doing something wrong. But when they do, we correct them. We do this because we love them and want them to know right from wrong. Through correction and guidance, your children learn. But, no matter what they do, you are always there for them, and you always love them. This is the same way your Heavenly Father is with you. (Psalm 1:6) "For the Lord watches over the way of the righteous, but the way of the wicked will perish."

There are many times when dealing with the people of this world that you feel all alone, even in your own family. If you have been born again and the people around you are not, life can be very difficult and lonely at times. I have felt this way many times, but the Lord always shows me that I am not alone. As long as Jesus Christ is your Lord and Savior, His Holy Spirit is always with you. (John 14:16) "And I will ask the Father, and He will give you another Counselor to be with you forever-- the Spirit of Truth." With the Spirit of Jesus living within your heart, you are never alone. All you have to do is call on Him and He will give you peace. (John: 14:27) "Peace I leave with you; My peace I give you. I do not give to you as the world gives. Do not let your hearts be troubled and do not be afraid."

When I feel the presence of the Lord I am more content than at any other time. Our precious Lord and Savior is always there for us. Sometimes you feel so down that you don't even feel like praying, I know this as well. But trust me, just call out His name and the rest gets easier. (Psalm 145:18) "The Lord is near to all who call on Him, to all who call on Him in truth." As you do this you will find you enjoy every moment you have with Him. The Lord Jesus Christ doesn't pressure you, get irritated with you, or put you down like so many people do. He is the best friend you will ever have. (Proverbs 18:24) "A man of many companions may come to ruin, but there is a friend who sticks closer than a brother."

The Israelites traveled from Egypt to the land of Canaan, and God was always with them. They sinned against Him time and time again, and God still stayed with them. That is love! He will be with you and guide you, but you are the one who must yield to Him and let Him guide you. He loves you so much; He does not want to make you love Him.

But if you do, He will bless you, take care of you, and supply all your needs as long as you love, trust, and obey Him. (Isaiah 58:11) "The Lord will guide you always; He will satisfy your needs in a sun-scorched land and will strengthen your frame." This means even when you are going through a rough trial and you are feeling weak and overwhelmed, trust God to strengthen you and be with you through it all. (Psalm 118:6) "The Lord is with me; I will not be afraid. What can man do to me?"

Has there ever been a time in your life when you felt completely abandoned by the Lord and felt alone? I have felt that many times before the salvation of my husband. It was several years of living with him and his alcohol and drug addictions before he accepted Jesus Christ. It was not easy, but I am a very stubborn person. I was determined that no matter what it took, no matter how long it took, I was not going to let Satan have my husband or my family. They are mine! They mean more to me than a few very, very rough years of praying and believing for their salvation. It was extremely hard. He put me down because of my faith and got angry with me because I no longer wanted to go out drinking with him. I felt very alone at times. I was still new as a Christian and my faith was still growing. But God showed me through a friend that I was not alone and that He did not abandon me. A friend that I worked with, one in which God used to convict me to change my ways and accept Him, came to me at work one morning after an especially difficult night with my husband. She came into my office and told me that she did not know why, but she felt that she had to tell me "God has not abandoned you." I was amazed! She didn't know that through her, God had strengthened my faith that day. I had just prayed the night before and asked God, why have you abandoned me?" I told her why I was so overjoyed at that moment and we both praised God together!

When you accept Jesus Christ, you must love, trust, and obey Him. As you do this, God will lead you, guide you, and supply all your needs. (Proverbs 16:7) "When a man's ways are pleasing to the Lord, He makes even his enemies live at peace with him." Putting God first as we are called to do helps you to be a better wife or husband. Until they are saved, they don't always see this. But, you can't have it both ways. You can't live according to the world and be a child of God. (I John 2:15-16) "Do not love the world or anything in the world. If anyone loves the world, the love of the Father is not in him. For everything in the world-- the cravings of sinful man, the lust of his eyes and the boasting of what he has and does--comes not from the Father but from the world." You cannot be a Christian and live according to the way God wants you to, a way pleasing to Him, and live according to the lusts and desires of the world. (I Corinthians 10:21-22) "You cannot drink the cup of the Lord and the cup of demons too; you cannot have a part in both the Lord's Table and the table of demons. Are we trying to arouse the Lord's jealousy? Are we stronger than He?"

God tells us that when we receive Jesus Christ, we are to be holy. (I Peter 1:13) "Be holy, because I am holy." We are to leave our sinful ways behind. (Deuteronomy 7:5-6) "This is what you are to do to them: Break down their altars, smash their sacred stones, cut down their Asherah poles, and burn their idols in the fire. For you are a people holy to the Lord your God." In other words, anything that you are addicted to, or any person or place that you put before your true worship of the Lord your God, is your idol.

You are only to have one master, and that is your Heavenly Father. (II Peter 2:19) "For a man is a slave to whatever has mastered him." As long as you are a child of God, He will always be with you. (Joshua 1:5) "I will never leave you nor forsake you." When you go through a problem that you just can't see a way through, remember that God has already been there ahead of you and will guide you, but you have to ask. (Isaiah 43:1-3) "Fear not, for I have redeemed you; I have summoned you by name; you are Mine. When you pass through the waters, I will be with you; and when you pass through the rivers, they will not sweep over you. When you walk through the fire, you will not be burned; the flames will not set you ablaze. For I am the Lord, your God, the Holy One of Israel, your Savior."

The trials you go through are to mold you and help you grow as a Christian, but your Heavenly Father will always protect you. (Psalm

23:4) "Even though I walk through the valley of the shadow of death, I will fear no evil, for You are with me."

God will walk through the fires of your trials with you and He will protect you as He did with Shadrach, Meshach, and Abednego in the book of Daniel. Some of King Nebuchadnezzar's officials set a trap for them. They proclaimed in (Daniel 3:4-5) "This is what you are commanded to do, O peoples, nations and men of every language: As soon as you hear the sound of the horn, flute, zither, lyre, harp, pipes and all kinds of music, you must fall down and worship the image of gold that King Nebuchadnezzar has set up. Whoever does not fall down and worship will immediately be thrown into a blazing furnace." They could not do it. They worshiped God alone. They believed that God was able to save them and He did. As they would not fall down and worship the image of gold, King Nebuchadnezzar gave orders to have them thrown into the furnace. The flames were so hot, that just being near them, they killed the soldiers who took the three men and threw them into the fire.

The king was amazed as he saw them walking around in the fire unharmed and with a fourth man in there as well. (Daniel 3:24-25) "Weren't there three men that we tied up and threw into the fire? They replied, Certainly, O king. He said, Look! I see four men walking around in the fire, unbound and unharmed, and the fourth looks like a son of the gods." As the Lord Jesus Christ was there for them, He will be there for you as well. (Psalm 139:5-12) "You hem me in--behind and before; You have laid Your hand upon me. Such knowledge is too wonderful for me, too lofty for me to attain. Where can I go from Your Spirit? Where can I flee from Your presence? If I go up to the heavens, You are there; if I make my bed in the depths, You are there. If I rise on the wings of the dawn, if I settle on the far side of the sea, even there Your hand will guide me, Your right hand will hold me fast. If I say, 'Surely the darkness will hide me and the light become night around me,' even the darkness will not be dark to You; the night will shine like the day, for darkness is as light to You." When you are a child of God, He will always be with you and His hand of protection will always be on you. Isn't that an awesome thought?

I have been through a lot of rough times, but I do admit I have learned a lot. I learn more and more with each passing day and each trial that comes my way. Through them all, I learn more and more about the depths of the Father's love and how He is with me through them all. (Ephesians 3:17-19) "And I pray that you, being rooted and established in love, may have power, together with all the saints, to grasp how wide and long and high and deep is the love of Christ, and know this love that surpasses knowledge--that you may be filled to the measure of all the fullness of God."

7

∾

Joy & Peace

Joy and peace are other ways in which God shows His love for us. Amid all your troubles you can still have joy and peace in your heart with Jesus Christ as your personal Lord and Savior. Being human you are still going to be sad and get discouraged from time to time, but you can still have peace in your heart. Peace in knowing that you are saved from eternal damnation, peace in knowing that no matter what you are going through, God is always there for you, and He will always love you. (Psalm 29:11) "The Lord gives strength to His people; the Lord blesses His people with peace."

In my own experience, before I came to the Lord, I felt as if I was carrying a ton of bricks around weighing down my heart. When I received Jesus into my heart, I found that the more I kept my eyes on Jesus, the more peace and joy within my heart I felt. (Isaiah 26:3) "You will keep in perfect peace him whose mind is steadfast because he trusts in you." As you may know, the more you read the Bible and put it into practice, the stronger your faith grows. (Romans 10:17) "Consequently, faith comes from hearing the message, and the message is heard through the Word of Christ." This is just like anything or anyone that you spend a lot of time with, the more time you spend with someone and get to know him or her, the more you love him or her. The more time you devote to God, you will find out just how much your Heavenly Father loves you.

Calvary should explain that all by itself. But Satan is the author of confusion and he tries to make you believe that God could never love you. This is not so. He gave his One and Only Son to pay the price for our sins! How much more convincing do you need? To top it off it is a gift, free! No one else in the world would do that! As you spend time with God you will find the closer you get to Him, the closer He will get to you. (James 4:8) "Come near to God and He will come near to you." Receiving Jesus Christ into your heart washes your sins away. You are now the righteousness of God in Christ Jesus. (II Corinthians 5:21) "God made Him who had no sin to be sin for us so that in Him we might become the righteousness of God." In receiving this you receive the fruit of His Spirit, in which peace and joy are only a portion of the fruit of His Spirit. (Isaiah 32:17) "The fruit of righteousness will be peace; the effect of righteousness will be quietness and confidence forever."

When you seek the Lord and do His will, you will see that He will always be there for you. Knowing this will bring you peace. You can have everyone around on your back for one thing or another and still have peace in your heart because you know that God will get you through everything. That is a promise straight from God. Isn't that awesome? (Psalm 9:10) "Those who know Your name will trust in You, for You, Lord, have never forsaken those who seek You."

You may think that it is impossible to have peace when you are suffering and hurting badly from some sort of loss, whether the loss is physical, financial, or from the loss of a loved one. Even in times of overwhelming pain and grief, you can still have peace. I know this from experience as well.

When I lost my 16-year-old son, I thought that my world was going to come to an end. I wanted to go with him. The pain was just too bad. He was such a loving child. He was very soft-hearted. I miss him very much, and this is difficult to write about, but knowing him, if it can help someone understand God's love, he would be very pleased. I thought that my heart was breaking into a million pieces. But all the while, it never shattered. God was holding it together. He would not let me fall apart. He was there for me then and still is. It is hard to explain, you would have to know from experience, but it felt as if God Himself was holding my heart in His hands and keeping me together. (Psalm 34:18) "The Lord is close to the brokenhearted and saves those who are crushed in spirit." (Psalm 147:3) "He heals the brokenhearted and binds up their wounds." Through all that pain, and pain I still live with, I still have peace.

Having peace through all situations in life becomes very noticeable to the people around you. If they do not know Jesus as their personal Lord and Savior, they will wonder, especially if they know of the troubles you may have, and why you always seem to be at peace. This brings glory to God. This is a great opening to witness, which we should all do, and are called to do.

When you have something wonderful, don't you want to share it? Knowing that someone you love might go to hell is not very comforting. As a child of God, we are the salt of the earth and should want our loved ones and friends who are not saved to come to the saving knowledge of Jesus Christ. (Matthew 5:13) "You are the salt of the earth." If no one ever witnessed, how would anyone get saved? (Matthew 28:19-20) "Therefore go and make disciples of all nations, baptizing them in the name of the Father and of the Son and of the Holy Spirit, and teaching them to obey everything I have commanded you. And surely I am with you always, to the very end of the age."

Through every situation that may come your way, you can be content and filled with the love of Jesus Christ that brings you peace and joy. (I Peter 1: 6-9) "In this, you greatly rejoice, though now for a little while you may have had to suffer grief in all kinds of trials. These have come so that your faith--of greater worth than gold, which perishes even though refined by fire--may be proved genuine and may result in praise, glory, and honor when Jesus Christ is revealed. Though you have not seen Him, you love Him; and even though you do not see Him now, you believe in Him and are filled with an inexpressible and glorious joy, for you are receiving the goal of your faith, the salvation of your souls." God will not put more on you than you can handle.

When you get weary and burdened all you have to do is come to Him. He will give you peace and rest. (Matthew 11:28-30) "Come to me, all you who are weary and burdened, and I will give you rest. Take My yoke upon you and learn from Me, for I am gentle and humble in heart, and you will find rest for your souls. For My yoke is easy and My burden is light." This verse is for the weary soul of the sinner, welcoming you to receive Jesus into your heart, but it is also for the child of God going through a difficult trial. Call out to God and He will give you rest.

Call out to God, in prayer, believing that He loves you and will answer your prayers. Whether it is a prayer for a loved one or a burden that has been laid upon your shoulders, God will hear and answer you and give you peace that tells you that He will answer your prayers. (Philippians 4: 6-7) "Do not be anxious about anything, but in everything, by prayer and petition, with thanksgiving, present your requests to God. And the peace of God, which transcends all understanding, will guard your hearts and your minds in Christ Jesus."

Paul wrote 13 of the 27 books in the New Testament, 5 of which were written from prison. How many of us could be confined to a prison cell and do the work of the Lord? If you truly love and trust the Lord as he did, you could. (Philippians 4:11-13) "For I have learned to be content whatever the circumstances. I know what it is to be in need, and I know what it is to have plenty. I have learned the secret of being content in any and every situation, whether well-fed or hungry, whether living in plenty or in want. I can do everything through Him who gives me strength."

In loving and obeying God, you will find favor with Him and He will bless you and give you peace and joy. (Leviticus 26:3-6) "If you follow My decrees and are careful to obey My commands, I will send you rain in its season, and the ground will yield its crops and the trees of the field their fruit. Your threshing will continue until the grape harvest and the grape harvest will continue until planting, and you will eat all the food you want and live in safety in your land. I will grant you peace in the land, and you will lie down and no one will make you afraid." In other words, as long as you love the Lord your God with all your heart and submit to His will, and obey His Word, He will take care of you. You will have a home to live in, the ability to work, and plenty of it. In having plenty of work your finances will be taken care of, and most of all you will have peace. (Acts 14:17) "He has shown kindness by giving you rain from heaven and crops in their seasons; He provides you with plenty of food and fills your heart with joy."

The Lord is the joy of our salvation. Having trust in Him will bring you peace and contentment. (Psalm 19:8) "The precepts of the Lord are right, giving joy to the heart." But the greatest joy of all is when we look into our Savior's face. For that is the day that we will have peace and joy everlasting for all eternity. (Isaiah 51:11) "The ransomed of the Lord will return. They will enter Zion with singing; everlasting joy will crown their heads. Gladness and joy will overtake them, and sorrow and sighing will flee away."

8

Trust & Faith

(**H**ebrews 11:1) "Now faith is being sure of what we hope for and certain of what we do not see." As you recognize that you are a sinner, ask forgiveness for your sins, and receive Jesus into your heart, you become a child of God. As a child of God, saved by grace you have peace with the Father, knowing that by the blood of Jesus Christ, He has purified your heart. You can go to Him with confidence in knowing that He loves you. (Romans 5:1-2) "Therefore, since we have been justified through faith, we have peace with God through our Lord Jesus Christ, through whom we have gained access by faith into this grace in which we now stand. And we rejoice in the hope of the glory of God."

You are saved by grace. Through that grace and the love of your Heavenly Father, He gives you faith and trust in Him. This is another way in which He shows His love for us. (Romans 12:3) "For by the grace given me I say to every one of you: Do not think of yourself more highly than you ought, but rather think of yourself with sober judgment, in accordance with the measure of faith God has given you." As you read the Word of God and do His will your faith will grow. (Romans 10:17) "Consequently faith comes from hearing the message, and the message is heard through the Word of Christ."

As you go through trials your faith is increased as you learn that God is there for you and wants the best for you. Even in difficult times, God does understand if at times your faith is weak. For someone who is a new Christian, the Lord will show in ways special to you, that He is there for you to build up your faith. Even the disciples had trouble with that and they lived with Jesus. (Luke 17:5-6) "The apostles said to the Lord, 'Increase our faith!' He replied, 'If you have faith as small as a mustard seed, you can say to this mulberry tree, 'Be uprooted and planted in the sea,' and it will obey you."

Your faith and trust in God will bring you peace. Where there is complete trust, there is no worry and where there is no worry, there is peace. (Romans 15:13) "May the God of hope fill you with all joy and peace as you trust in Him, so that you may overflow with hope by the power of the Holy Spirit." As you trust in God you will know that He will always be there to lead and guide you in all circumstances. (Proverbs 3:5-6) "Trust in the Lord with all your heart and lean not on your own understanding; in all your ways acknowledge Him, and He will make your paths straight."

As you trust in the Lord you will know that you can cast all your burdens on the Lord and He will take care of them. He does this because He loves you. (Psalm 55:22) "Cast all your cares on the Lord and He will sustain you, He will never let the righteous fall." (Isaiah 46:4) "Even to your old age and gray hairs I am He, I am He who will sustain you. I have made you and I will carry you; I will sustain you and I will rescue you." Through every burden you have, you know that you can go to the Lord with confidence in knowing that He will help you. What an awesome show of love! God promises to take care of your needs, all you have to do is love, trust, and obey Him. His work seems to be a whole lot harder because, talking from experience we sure can make a mess out of things. (Psalm 68:19) "Praise be to the Lord, to God our Savior, who daily bears our burdens."

Our Lord Jesus Christ understands weakness. As He prayed in the Garden of Gethsemane the night that He was betrayed, He felt the overwhelming weight on His shoulders of what He was about to undertake. This troubled Him greatly as He prayed in (Matthew 26:39), "My Father if it is possible, may this cup be taken from Me. Yet not as I will, but as you will." Yet He still submitted to the Father's will. This helps Him understand the weaknesses that we feel from time to time.

In fixing our eyes on Jesus, and on what we know from the promises He gives us in the Bible, He will give you peace and see you through your trials. (Hebrews 12:2-3) "Let us fix our eyes on Jesus, the author and perfecter of our faith, who for the joy set before Him endured the cross, scorning its shame, and sat down at the right hand of the throne of God. Consider Him who endured such opposition from sinful men, so that you will not grow weary and lose heart."

The trials you go through will strengthen your faith as you see that your Heavenly Father is there for you and gives you the wisdom and understanding that you need to mature as a Christian and overcome your trials. (James 1:2-5) "Consider it pure joy, my brothers, whenever you face trials of many kinds because you know that the testing of your faith develops perseverance. Perseverance must finish its work so that you may be mature and complete, not lacking anything. If any of you lacks wisdom, he should ask God, who gives generously to all without finding fault, and it will be given to him."

Our Heavenly Father lets trials come your way for your good, they are to mold you and to change you into a mature Christian. (Jeremiah 18:6) "O house of Israel, can I not do with you as this potter does?" declares the Lord. "Like clay in the hands of the potter, so are you in My hand, O house of Israel." Although trials and tribulations may come your way, to mold you and strengthen your faith, it is because of the unending love of God the Almighty Father. He wants to bless you and to prosper you. (Jeremiah 29:11) "For I know the plans I have for you," declares the Lord, "plans to prosper you and not to harm you, plans to give you hope and a future." (Romans 8:28) "And we know that in all things God works for the good of those who love Him, who have been called according to His purpose."

Through experience, from the trials that you face, you learn, grow, and your heart changes. (Ezekiel 36:26) "I will give you a new heart and put a new spirit in you; I will remove from you your heart of stone and give you a heart of flesh." This is from the abundant love that God has for us. (Romans 5:1-5) "Therefore, since we have been justified through faith, we have peace with God through our Lord Jesus Christ, through whom we have gained access by faith into this grace in which we now stand. And we rejoice in the hope of the glory of God. Not only so, but we also rejoice in our sufferings, because we know that suffering produces perseverance, perseverance, character; and character, hope. And hope does not disappoint us, because God has poured out His love into our hearts by the Holy Spirit, whom He has given us."

God will help you along the way as you pray and ask for His help when your faith is weak. Just as you want your children to love and trust you, so does God want us to love and trust Him. We show our children that we love them. When they come to you from time to time and ask you, "Mommy (or daddy), do you love me?" You tell them you do and you show them by taking care of them, and by giving them things that make them happy. Your Heavenly Father wants to do the same. (Matthew 7:7-11) "Ask and it will be given to you; seek and you will find; knock and the door will be opened to you. For everyone who asks receives; he who seeks finds; and to him who knocks, the door will be opened. Which of you, if his son asks for bread, will give him a stone? Or if he asks for a fish, will give him a snake? If you, then, though you are evil, know how to give good gifts to your children, how much more will your Father in heaven give good gifts to those who ask Him!"

We are God's children. As Jesus suffered and then rose to His glory, being children of God we are joint heirs and will share in His glory as long as we persevere and don't give up. (Romans 8:15-17) "For you did not receive a spirit of fear, but you received the Spirit of sonship. And by Him, we cry, 'Abba, Father.' The Spirit Himself testifies with our spirit that we are God's children. Now if we are children, then we are heirs-- heirs of God and co-heirs with Christ, if indeed we share in His sufferings in order that we may also share in His glory."

Your faith and trust in Him will help you overcome your trials with victory! Faith pleases God! (Hebrews 11:6) "And without faith it is impossible to please God because anyone who comes to Him must believe that He exists and that He rewards those who earnestly seek Him." In Matthew 15:21-28, Jesus walked through Tyre and Sidon and a Canaanite woman came to Him and asked Him to deliver her daughter. Her daughter was demon-possessed. Her faith pleased Jesus and He healed her daughter. (Matthew 15:28) "Woman, you have great faith! Your request is granted."

Our Heavenly Father, out of His unending love grants you the gift of salvation through our Lord Jesus Christ. He also answers prayers and works out miracles in you and your loved ones. (Galatians 3:5) "Does God give you His Spirit and work miracles among you because you observe the Law, or because you believe what you heard?" All of this is through faith. Through faith, you are blessed. (Galatians 3:6-9) "Consider Abraham: 'He believed God, and it was credited to him as righteousness.' Understand, then, that those who believe are children of Abraham. The Scripture foresaw that God would justify the Gentiles by faith, and announced the gospel in advance to Abraham: 'All nations will be blessed through you.' So those who have faith are blessed along with Abraham, the man of faith."

Through faith in Jesus, we have eternal life. We are all united as brothers and sisters in Christ. (Galatians 3:26-29) "You are all sons of God through faith in Jesus Christ, for all of you who were baptized into Christ have clothed yourselves with Christ. There is neither Jew nor Greek, slave nor free, male nor female, for you are all one in Christ Jesus. If you belong to Christ, then you are Abraham's seed, and heirs according to the promise."

Out of God's love for us, He gives the blessings of His grace. Out of our love and faith in Him, we receive it. (Psalm 138:6-8) "Though the Lord is on high, He looks upon the lowly, but the proud He knows from afar. Though I walk in the midst of trouble, You preserve my life; You stretch out Your hand against the anger of my foes, with Your right hand You save me. The Lord will fulfill His purpose for me; Your love, O Lord, endures forever-do not abandon the works of Your hands." (Galatians 5:5-6) "But by faith we eagerly await through the Spirit the righteousness for which we hope. For in Christ Jesus, neither circumcision nor uncircumcision has any value. The only thing that counts is faith expressing itself through love."

9

Blessings

(Revelation 22:14) "Blessed are those who wash their robes, that they may have the right to the tree of life and may go through the gates into the city." Blessings from the Lord are a wonderful showing of God's love, but nothing can compare to the gift of eternal life. He gave us His One and Only Son to be the atoning sacrifice for our sins! That should be blessing enough for us all since there is no one here on earth who can live up to the righteousness of God on their own merits. It is when He purifies your heart that you receive the best blessing of all. The peace and assurance in your heart that tells you that your sins are forgiven and you have received the gift of His salvation. (Psalm 24:4-5) "He who has clean hands and a pure heart, who does not lift up his soul to an idol or swear by what is false. He will receive blessing from the Lord and vindication from God his Savior."

Without the gift of salvation, all else is meaningless; with Jesus Christ as your personal Lord and Savior, your righteousness will shine with the love of Jesus from within your heart. (Psalm 37:6) "He will make your righteousness shine like the dawn, the justice of your cause like the noon-day sun."

God knows that with the sinful nature within us, which goes back to Adam and Eve, without His help and guidance, we would all be doomed to eternal damnation. We would be separated from Him forever. For that reason, He sent Jesus Christ to pay the price for our sins for us! Through receiving Jesus Christ, you also receive the Holy Spirit. This is a true blessing of love. (Galatians 3:13-14) "Christ redeemed us from the curse of the Law by becoming a curse for us, for it is written, 'Cursed is everyone who is hung on a tree.' He redeemed us in order that the bless-ing given to Abraham might come to the Gentiles through Christ Jesus so that by faith we might receive the promise of the Spirit." The Holy Spirit comforts, guides, and intercedes. (John 14:26) "But the Counselor, the Holy Spirit, whom the Father will send in My name, will teach you all things and will remind you of everything I have said to you."

We all experience and receive God's love, but no one knows how wide and how deep the Father's love is. I know for myself, that He is always doing something that truly amazes me. Not in what He does, it is the love that He shows me in what He does that amazes me. There are times that He will do something for me and I feel like I just don't deserve it. But that is what the Father's love is all about. He loves us because He wants to and not because of anything we do or don't do. (Ephesians 3:17-18) "And I pray that you, being rooted and established in love, may have power, together with all the saints, to grasp how wide and long and high and deep is the love of Christ, and to know this love that surpasses knowledge--that you may be filled to the measure of all the fullness of God."

Time and time again I mess things up and the emotions of this world get the best of me. Satan knows how to blindside you and attack you before you know what is hitting you. I have gotten angry with God and doubted Him. Then, the Lord will show me just how much He loves me. He usually picks me back up through a friend, Joelle. She will call and get me back on track. If I am having a "pity party" or my faith took a nosedive due to something painful at home, she will give me a verse from the Bible and it will speak right to my heart. I know it is from God. He speaks to all of us through His Word and through the people around us. I will ask His forgiveness for my sin or attitude, and He gives me peace in my heart that tells me He loves me and forgives me. (Matthew 5:7)

"Blessed are the merciful, for they will be shown mercy." His mercy and understanding are a blessing from the Lord that I know I could not live without. (Psalm 2:12) "Blessed are all who take refuge in Him." (Luke 1:50) "His mercy extends to those who fear Him, from generation to generation."

God blesses us in many different ways. Abraham was in His old age when God told Him He would have a son. Most of us would think, "How can that be?" But Abraham believed Him, and He was 86 years old when He became a father to Ishmael. (Genesis 15:6) "Abraham believed the Lord, and He credited to Him as righteousness." Abraham feared the Lord and trusted Him. (Psalm 128:1-4) "Blessed are all who fear the Lord, who walk in His ways. You will eat the fruit of your labor; blessings and prosperity will be yours. Your wife will be like a fruitful vine within your house; your sons will be like olive shoots around your table. Thus, is the man blessed who fears the Lord."

The Lord blessed him and his descendants after him because of this. (Genesis 17:4-7) "As for Me, this is My covenant with you: You will be the father of many nations. No longer will you be called Abram, your name will be Abraham, for I have made you a father of many nations. I will make you very fruitful; I will make nations of you, and kings will come from you. I will establish My covenant as an everlasting covenant between Me and you and your descendants after you for the generations to come, to be your God and the God of your descendants after you."

Children are a gift from God. Watching my children grow from precious little babies into loving children has brought me great joy. I would not change one minute with them. Seeing them grow, and the different personalities they each have brings such enjoyment. I feel sorry for anyone who is married and has no children. There have been many times when I was having a bad day and one of my two boys would come up to me, hug me, and tell me that he loved me. Seeing their loving little faces and being so sincere picked me back up instantly. (Psalm 127:3-4) "Sons are a heritage from the Lord, children a reward from Him. Like arrows in the hands of a warrior are sons born in one's youth."

As a child of God, you are called to be obedient to Him. As you obey and trust Him, God blesses you even more! He supplies all your needs and protects you from harm. This includes a roof over your head, food, and clothing. (Deuteronomy 28:1-8) "If you fully obey the Lord your God and carefully follow all His commands I give you today, the Lord your God will set you high above all the nations on earth. All these blessings will come upon you and accompany you if you obey the Lord your God: You will be blessed in the city and blessed in the country. The fruit of your womb will be blessed, and the crops of your land and the young of your livestock--the calves of your herds and the lambs of your flocks. Your basket and your kneading trough will be blessed. You will be blessed when you come in and blessed when you go out. The Lord will grant that the enemies who rise up against you will be defeated before you. They will come at you from one direction but flee from you in seven. The Lord will send a blessing on your barns and on everything you put your hands to. The Lord your God will bless you in the land He is giving you."

In the Book of Exodus chapter 25, the Bread of the Presence is described. The Israelites were to keep 12 loaves of bread, representing the 12 tribes of Israel, before the Lord at all times. This was the daily share of the priests. This represents how God provides for His pastors, priests, and ministers through His people. This also represents Jesus, who is the "Bread of Life," supplying all of our needs, spiritually and physically.

In blessing you with a home and food, this also means that he blesses you with the ability to acquire these things. He gives you the talent and inspiration you need to be good at whatever you do in life. (Deuteronomy 8:18) "But remember the Lord your God, for it is He who gives you the ability to produce wealth, and so confirms His covenant, which He swore to your forefathers, as it is today."

The Lord your God wants to give to you in abundance. He does not want you to need anything. He is your Heavenly Father. As you want to supply all the needs and wants of your children, so does God want to supply your needs. (Psalm 65:11) "You crown the year with your bounty, and your carts overflow with abundance." (Joshua 1:8) "Do not let the Book of the Law depart from your mouth; meditate on it day and night, so that you may be careful to do everything written in it. Then you will be prosperous and successful."

In supplying all of your needs and blessing you, you are to share with others who are in need, giving to them as God gives to you. This is another way in which God blesses His people. He does it through you and me. (Romans 12:13) "Share with God's people who are in need. Practice hospitality." In the Book of Acts, as the Apostles preached the good news of Jesus, more and more people were baptized into the family of God. They were filled with the Holy Spirit. They were united as brothers and sisters in Christ and of one heart and mind as we all should be. (Acts 4:32) "All the believers were one in heart and mind. No one claimed that any of his possessions was his own, but they shared everything they had."

For those of us who have children, you know that there will always be some sort of illness or pain that they will endure. You are always there for them to make them feel better and put bandages on their wounds. This is another blessing from the Lord. He also promises to heal us and comfort us when we are brokenhearted. (Exodus 15:26) "For I am the Lord, who heals you." He heals our bodies as well as our hearts. (Psalm 147:3) "He heals the brokenhearted and binds up their wounds." (Psalm 34:18) "The Lord is close to the brokenhearted and saves those who are crushed in spirit." I know this only too well. The Lord picked up the pieces of my heart when my son died, and then 2 years later when my mother passed away. He picked up the pieces of my broken heart and glued it back together with the abundance of His love. The pain is still there, for I will always miss them, but God is always there to comfort me.

God also blesses you as you go through the trials of life. As you persevere and don't give up He will answer your prayers along the way. (Psalm 145: 18-19) "The Lord is near to all who call on Him, to all who call on Him in truth. He fulfills the desires of those who fear Him; He hears their cry and saves them." As you make it through your trials He blesses you with the plans He has for you. (Job 8:7) "Your beginnings will seem humble, so prosperous will your future be." In obeying the Lord your God, loving and trusting Him, and persevering through your trials, knowing that He is in control, you will be blessed by God; not only in this life; but also in the one to come. (James 1:12) "Blessed is the man who perseveres under trial because when he has stood the test, he will receive the crown of life that God has promised to those who love Him."

Your Heavenly Father also understands that it is hard to go through life without messing up while living here on earth. But in making mistakes and sinning, you must also reap what you sow. When you say something that hurts someone or do something wrong, there are always consequences for every action. Your finances might take a tumble downhill or people you have hurt seem to make themselves scarce. (Malachi 3:5-6) "So I will come near to you for judgment. I will be quick to testify against sorcerers, adulterers, and perjurers, against those who defraud laborers of their wages, who oppress the widows and the fatherless, and deprive aliens of justice, but do not fear Me,' says the Lord Almighty. 'I the Lord do not change. So you, O descendants of Jacob, are not destroyed."

In sinning against the Lord, you will be judged by Him and disciplined as any parent disciplines their children when they do something wrong. Some or all of your blessings might fall away, depending on how long it takes you to see the error of your ways and repent. But when you return to the Lord and ask forgiveness, He will restore to you the blessings that you lost due to your disobedience in sinning. (Deuteronomy 30:2-3) "And when you and your children return to the Lord your God and obey Him with all your heart and with all your soul according to everything I command you today, then the Lord your God will restore your fortunes and have compassion on you and gather you again from all the nations where He scattered you."

Another way in which God blesses you and meets your needs is by obeying His command to tithe. In not tithing, you are robbing God and not trusting Him to provide your needs. (Malachi 3:8-12) "Will a man rob God? Yet you rob Me. But you ask, 'How do we rob you?' In tithes and offerings. You are under a curse--the whole nation of you--because you are robbing Me. Bring the whole tithe into the storehouse, that there may be food in My house. Test Me in this,' says the Lord Almighty, 'and see if I will not throw open the floodgates of heaven and pour out so much blessing that you will not have room enough for it. I will prevent pests from devouring your crops, and the vines in your fields will not cast their fruit,' says the Lord Almighty. 'Then all the nations will call you blessed, for yours will be a delightful land,' says the Lord Almighty."

In traveling down the road of life, the path gets rough at times, but God is always there for you. He loves you and wants to bless you, to forgive you, and to give you the grace of His salvation. (Psalm 103:2-5) "Praise the Lord, O my soul, and forget not all His benefits--who forgives all your sins and heals all your diseases, who redeems your life from the pit and crowns you with love and compassion, who satisfies your desires with good things so that your youth is renewed like the eagle's."

10

Protection

(Psalm 23:4) "Even though I walk through the valley of the shadow of death, I will fear no evil, for You are with me; Your rod and Your staff; they comfort me." Because of God's undying love for us, He will always be there to comfort and protect us. Since God created the world, He is Sovereign over it and everything in it. (Acts 4:24) "Sovereign Lord, they said, you made the heaven and the earth and the sea, and everything in them." (Romans 8:31) "What, then, shall we say in response to this? If God is for us, who can be against us?" As long as you are a child of God, you should 'fear no evil,' because our God is a God of love, but He is also strong and powerful. (I John 4:4) "You, dear children, are from God and have overcome them because the One who is in you is greater than the one who is in the world."

There will always be fearful situations as long as evil exists in the world, but with God as your Father, there is nothing to fear. (Joshua 4:24) "He did this so that all the peoples of the earth might know that the hand of the Lord is powerful and so that you might always fear the Lord your God." God is not a dictator. He is a God of love. This is why He gave man free will. He wants you to love and trust Him of your own free will. The love given freely is a love worth having. For this reason, there are people in the world who are not a child of God and fall under Satan's spells all too easily. When this happens, God's people get tormented, attacked, and hurt. But fear not, for the Lord your God is always there to save you. (Hebrews 13:6) "So we say with confidence, 'The Lord is my helper; I will not be afraid. What can man do to me?"

There are evil forces in the world as long as Satan still roams the earth. But remember, there is nothing stronger or more powerful than God. Satan is strong and powerful, and you do not want to go up against him without God as your Father, you will surely lose the battle. But with God as your Father, you can always rely on Him for protection. He is the Creator of all things and is more powerful than Satan. There is nothing in the world that is stronger than the Lord your God.   (Deuteronomy 7:17-18) "You may say to yourselves, 'These nations are stronger than we are. How can we drive them out?' But remember well what the Lord your God did to Pharaoh and to all Egypt."

As the Israelites left Egypt, Pharaoh's heart hardened once again. He and his army followed behind to bring them back. But God's hand of protection was on them. He dried up the Red Sea and the Israelites traveled through it all night. God kept Pharaoh's army away from them and kept it night on the Egyptian side, and full light on the side of the Israelites. As they crossed through the Red Sea to the other side, God let the Egyptians through. They followed the Israelites into the Red Sea and when all the Israelites were safe, God let the waters of the Red Sea sweep over the Egyptians, killing all of them. (Isaiah 43:1-3) "Fear not, for I have redeemed you; I have summoned you by name; you are mine. When you pass through the waters I will be with you; and when you pass through the rivers, they will not sweep over you. When you walk through the fire, you will not be burned; the flames will not set you ablaze. For I am the Lord, your God, the Holy One of Israel, your Savior."

God is our light in the darkness. In Him, there is no darkness. He will light your way and keep you from harm. (Psalm 18:28) "You, O Lord, keep my lamp burning; my God turns my darkness into light."

There are going to be times when someone or something scares you; in those times, call on the Lord. He loves you and will be there for you. (I John 4:18) "There is no fear in love. But perfect love drives out fear because fear has to do with punishment. The one who fears is not made perfect in love." As you call on the Lord in times of trouble, He will give you peace, a knowing deep within your heart that tells you that He is with you and that you are safe. (Psalm 4:8) "I will lie down and sleep in peace, for You alone, O Lord, make me dwell in safety."

In the Book of Joshua, Joshua sent out 2 spies into the land of Jericho to look over the land. They came to a prostitute's house by the name of Rahab. She hid the 2 spies and protected them until they could escape without being harmed. God's hand of protection was on them through her.

The Israelites were a 'Holy People.' Before we all accept Jesus through faith we are all 'unbelievers,' Rahab was and had heard about them, how God was with them and protected them. God put a fear on all the inhabitants in the land He promised to the Israelites and a fear of the Israelites. (Deuteronomy 11:25) "No man will be able to stand against you. The Lord your God, as He promised you, will put the terror and fear of you on the whole land, wherever you go." Through that fear, Rahab believed that God existed. Through that belief, she protected the spies and for that, when they came to take over the city, her and her family's lives were spared. (Psalm 27:1) "The Lord is my light and my salvation--whom shall I fear? The Lord is the stronghold of my life--of whom shall I be afraid?"

The Lord was her salvation and will be yours too. He will love and protect you and your family all the days of your life and throughout all of eternity if you put your love, trust, and faith in Him. (Psalm 37:28) "For the Lord loves the just and will not forsake His faithful ones. They will be protected forever, but the offspring of the wicked will be cut off."

Are you up against a battle and don't know where to turn? Or do you have loved ones in trouble and need God's protection? As God saved Rahab and her family, He will save yours too. In order to receive His protection and saving grace you must first receive Jesus. (Joel 2:32) "And everyone who calls on the name of the Lord will be saved." You must also believe in what you are praying for and pray without ceasing no matter how long it takes. (Matthew 21:22) "If you believe, you will receive whatever you ask for in prayer." You must also keep on praying and believing. God never promises immediate answers to our prayers. His time is not our time. He knows the best and the right time to answer your prayers. (Isaiah 62:7) "You who call on the Lord, give yourselves no rest, and give Him no rest till He establishes Jerusalem and makes her the praise of the earth."

When my oldest son was 7 months old, we were stationed in Germany. My husband was in the army. When people were getting ready to move back to the States, the army put them in special housing after their belongings were packed and shipped back to the States. We had some friends who were getting ready to go back to the States and the transition housing was all full. We let them stay with us. We lived in an army apartment building with concrete steps. It had four floors and we lived on the second. As they were bringing their luggage inside, I had to use the restroom badly. I asked my friend if she would watch Timmy for a minute.

Well, she didn't. She left him crawling around in his bedroom and went to help get more of their luggage in. She left the door open. I was only a minute, but sometimes that is all it takes. He was nowhere around and the door was open! I was overwhelmed with panic! A little voice told me to go upstairs. As I got to the top of the third floor, there sat my son in front of someone's door almost by the edge of the steps! When I saw him, I knew it was God who directed me to the third floor. It was God's hand of protection that was on my son as well. There is no way that a 7-month-old baby could climb up one flight of concrete stairs without getting hurt unless God was protecting him! I picked him up and held him so tight. I just couldn't let go.

How much more do you think your Heavenly Father wants to hold you and protect you in the same way? After all, the love that we have for our family and friends comes from Him. (I John 4:7) "Dear friends, let us love one another, for love comes from God." I knew then God was there watching over my family. (Psalm 121:5-8) "The Lord watches over you--the Lord is your shade at your right hand; the sun will not harm you by day, nor the moon by night. The Lord will keep you from all harm--He will watch over your life; the Lord will watch over your coming and going, both now and forevermore."

In the Book of I Samuel, the Israelites asked for a king to rule over them. This displeased God since He was their King. But He gave them what they wanted. The first king was Saul. It didn't take long before the position went to his head. He was disobedient in carrying out God's orders. This happened more than once. God told Samuel, the prophet, that He had chosen someone else to take Saul's place. He chose David. David was small in size. But with God being the one he submitted to and had faith in, made up for his small stature. Because of Saul's continued disobedience, the Spirit of the Lord left him.

"If My people would but listen to me, if Israel would follow my ways, how quickly would I subdue their enemies and turn My hand against their foes." (Psalm 81:13-14)

David went up against Goliath, a strong and powerful Philistine. With God fighting for him, David killed Goliath with one shot of his slingshot to Goliath's forehead. With God as your Savior, size does not matter. He grew very popular with the people as he conquered their enemies. This made Saul very jealous and he vowed to kill him. God's hand of protection never left David. No matter where David went there was always someone there which God used to protect him, even Saul's own son! God watched over David and protected him until the Philistines eventually killed Saul.

What God did for David, as you love, trust, and obey Him, He will do the same for you. I can't think of a better way to close this chapter than to end it with Psalm 91. It is a beautiful Scripture and if you let it, it will speak right to your heart.

"He who dwells in the shelter of the Most High will rest in the shadow of the Almighty. I will say of the Lord, 'He is my refuge and my fortress, my God, in whom I trust.' Surely He will save you from the fowler's snare and from the deadly pestilence. He will cover you with His feathers, and under His wings you will find refuge; His faithfulness will be your shield and rampart. You will not fear the terror of night, nor the arrow that flies by day, nor the pestilence that stalks in the darkness, nor the plague that destroys at midday. A thousand may fall at your side, ten thousand at your right hand, but it will not come near you. You will only observe with your eyes and see the punishment of the wicked. If you make the Most High your dwelling--even the Lord, who is my refuge-then no harm will befall you, no disaster will come near your tent. For He will command His angels concerning you to guard you in all your ways; they will lift you up in their hands, so that you will not strike your foot against a stone. You will tread upon the lion and the cobra; you will trample the great lion and the serpent. 'Because he loves me,' says the Lord, I will rescue him; I will protect him, for he acknowledges My name. He will call upon Me, and I will answer him; I will be with him in trouble, I will deliver him and honor him. With long life will I satisfy him and show him My salvation."

11

⌘

Answered Prayers & Deliverance

(**P**salm 34:15) "The eyes of the Lord are on the righteous and His ears are attentive to their cry." The Lord your God wants to answer your prayers. His eyes are on the righteous and He hears their prayers. This means you must be a child of God, saved through our Lord Jesus Christ. If you have not received His free gift of salvation through Jesus Christ, you are rejecting Him. Jesus died on the cross for our sins. (II Corinthians 5:21) "God made Him who had no sin to be sin for us so that in Him we might become the righteousness of God." If you are rejecting God and the enormous show of love He has for us, by sending Jesus to die on the cross and take our punishment for us, how can you expect God to answer your prayers? (Matthew 12:30) "He who is not with Me is against Me, and he who does not gather with Me scatters."

As described in the Book of Leviticus, the Israelites that brought sin offerings to the priests to offer up to the Lord had to bring them to the entrance of the Tent of Meeting. They had to be offered at the door of the Tabernacle. Jesus is our Tabernacle and He was our sin offering. The offering had to be done at the entrance because the Lord your God is holy, and no one can enter into the presence of God who has not been cleansed of his or her sins. Jesus is the one who purifies our sins. (I John 1:7) "But

64

if we walk in the light, as He is in the light, we have fellowship with one another, and the blood of Jesus, His Son, purifies us from all sin."

In the Book of Ezra, it tells of the Israelites through Cyrus, the king of Persia, trying to rebuild the Temple of the Lord. It had been torn down when they went into forced captivity in Babylon. Their enemies wrote a letter to King Artaxerxes to put a stop to it. It was temporarily stopped until King Darius issued an order to search the archives to find the original decree by King Cyrus. The order was found and the order to rebuild was given. King Artaxerxes even sent for Ezra, the priest, to come to Jerusalem from Babylon to instruct people on the Book of the Law and to appoint judges and magistrates. The construction began and the Israelites consecrated themselves to the Lord. But, it didn't take long for Satan to attack. The people began to intermarry with foreign women. This was forbidden. (Deuteronomy 7:3) "Do not intermarry with them."

We are not to be unequally yoked. (II Corinthians 6:14) "Do not be yoked together with unbelievers. For what do righteousness and wickedness have in common?" (II Corinthians 6:17) "Therefore come out from them and be separate, says the Lord. Touch no unclean thing, and I will receive you." We are to do this by receiving forgiveness of our sins. God is holy and we are to be holy. (I Peter 1:16) "Be holy, because I am holy." When you leave a life of sin, you are not to bring anything to cause you to sin into your household. These foreign women worshipped other gods. They brought their idols with them. They were giving Satan a foothold in their house by doing this. You play with fire and you will get burned. God was very displeased with them for this and Ezra wept bitterly before the Lord. In doing this he was praying for God's mercy. The people saw him weeping for their sins and were convicted by the Lord of their sins. They started confessing their sins. They cleansed themselves. They rid themselves of the foreign women and their idols and were made right in the eyes of the Lord. Ezra's sincere heartfelt prayer reached the Lord's ears and the people were convicted. His prayer was heard and answered.

Just as God led the Israelites into the Promised Land, He also wants to lead you into your promised land (answer your prayers). (Psalm 23:1-4)

"The Lord is my Shepherd; I shall not be in want. He makes me lie down in green pastures, He leads me beside quiet waters, and He restores my soul. He guides me in paths of righteousness for His name's sake. Even though I walk through the valley of the shadow of death, I will fear no evil, for You are with me; Your rod and Your staff, they comfort me."

This is another way in which our Heavenly Father shows His love for us: by answering our prayers. (Mark 11:24) "Therefore I tell you, whatever you ask for in prayer, believe that you have received it, and it will be yours." The Lord understands sometimes your faith is weak, rather than pray with unbelief, ask Him to help you with your doubt. (Mark 9:24) "Help me overcome my unbelief!"

As God heard the cry of the Israelites when they were in bondage to the Egyptians and delivered them, He hears your cry as well. They had to conquer and possess, trusting in God to deliver the enemy into their hands. We have to do something as well. We have to trust God to answer our prayers. We help to conquer by resisting the devil. (James 4:7-8) "Submit yourselves, then, to God. Resist the devil, and he will flee from you. Come near to God and He will come near to you." Satan will try to discourage you and make you feel down about yourself, especially if it takes a while for your prayers to be answered. But you must resist these thoughts, knowing that they are not from God. (II Corinthians 10:5) "We demolish arguments and every pretension that sets itself up against the knowledge of God, and we take captive every thought to make it obedient to Christ."

God wants to bless you; He does not discourage you. (James 1:17) "Every good and perfect gift is from above." The only way to truly resist the devil is to trust and obey God, and to read His Word daily. As you read His Word, your faith grows as you learn about the love and promises He has for you. Knowing His promises and trusting in them will give you the power to fight off Satan's attacks. Satan tried to keep the Israelites from possessing the Promised Land by the enemies that came their way. Some were bigger and stronger, and so are the trials that you are facing and answers that you are waiting on. But God is stronger. (Deuteronomy 9:3) "But be assured today that the Lord your God is the

One who goes across ahead of you like a devouring fire. He will destroy them; He will subdue them before you. And you will drive them out and annihilate them quickly, as the Lord has promised you."

You must believe in God's love for you and trust Him, knowing that He wants to answer your prayers. (Psalm 37:4) "Delight yourself in the Lord and He will give you the desires of your heart." As you pray, thank Him for it in advance, trusting Him to answer your prayer. A sacrifice is something hard for you to give up. That is what a sacrifice of praise is: praising and thanking God for the answer to your prayers when they haven't been answered yet. Thank Him and praise Him for the answer, for God delights in thanksgiving and faith. (Psalm 50:14-15) "Sacrifice thank offerings to God, fulfill your vows to the Most High, and call upon Me in the day of trouble; I will deliver you and you will honor Me."

One of the things that we all pray for is that our loved ones who are not saved would come to know the Lord as their personal Lord and Savior. God gave us free will and He says, (Revelation 3:20) "Here I am! I stand at the door and knock. If anyone hears My voice and opens the door, I will come in and eat with him and he with Me." We must accept Jesus of our own free will, but God knows that "knock at the door" that will bring them to their knees before Him. (Proverbs 16:9) "In his heart a man plans his course, but the Lord determines his steps." (Proverbs 19:21) "Many are the plans in a man's heart, but it is the Lord's purpose that prevails."

God will let things happen if it is for our good. (Job 33:29-30) "God does all these things to a man--twice, even three times--to turn back his soul from the pit that the light of life may shine on him." Just as He let trouble come Job's way, it was for his good. It was to test and strengthen his faith. God will let things happen to you and the loved ones that you are praying for if it benefits your soul. He let Satan take Job's children and finances away. Job passed the test and God gave him children again and twice as many animals. God did this for his good and blessed him for his perseverance. (Proverbs 16:4) "The Lord works out everything for His own ends--even the wicked for a day of disaster."

The Lord always acts with our best interest in mind, the most important being our souls and our eternal salvation and for His glory. God has a divine purpose and plan for us all. (II Timothy 1:8-9) "But join with me in suffering for the gospel, by the power of God, who has saved us and called us to a holy life--not because of anything we have done but because of His own purpose and grace." It is not for us to understand the ways of God, we just need to look to Jesus and every other blessing in our life and know that God loves us. Jesus should be enough in itself to show us God's abounding love for us. Anyone who loves that much can only want your good. (Micah 4:12) "But they do not know the thoughts of the Lord; they do not understand His plan, He who gathers them like sheaves to the threshing floor." We don't always understand the way that God answers some of our prayers, but trusting in His love will see you through and change your heart as you wait for your prayers to be answered. (John 15:16) "You did not choose me, but I chose you and appointed you to go and bear fruit--fruit that will last. Then the Father will give you whatever you ask in My name."

In the Book of I Kings, Elijah was staying with a widow whose son had died. She came to Elijah and cried out to him in despair. Elijah brought him up to his room and laid him on his bed. He cried out to God in prayer. He then laid out across the boy three times and prayed for the Lord to return the boy to life, God answered his prayers. True faith in God and His love will answer your prayers. (Psalm 3:8) "From the Lord comes deliverance. May your blessing be on your people."

It may look overwhelming and there is no way possible that someone that you are praying for will ever get saved. I thought that at first about my husband. Friends even told me, "He may never get saved!" But as I kept praying, God kept revealing Scriptures to me that had to do with praying for someone. He also revealed it to me in my spirit. I just had this "knowing" that he was going to be saved. No matter what anyone else said, I kept relying on the promises of God. It was a long and hard road, but God gave me the strength, love, and comfort that I needed to get through it. Things may look overwhelming, but nothing is too strong or impossible for God. (Psalm 147:5) "Great is our Lord and mighty in power; His understanding has no limit." Praise God! Today, although he is saved, he prayed to receive the Lord with me, and he went back to drinking again. I believe the pain of losing our son was just too great. God does answer the prayers of true faith. Nothing is beyond His reach and God will heal his broken heart.

In the Book of Numbers, as the Israelites got closer to the land of Canaan, they started complaining. They were tired of the manna. Moses cried out to the Lord in prayer. In His anger, because the people did not trust or appreciate Him, God told Moses that He would give them so much meat that they would be sick of it. Moses asked how we could have enough flocks and herds to do this. God's response to him was in (Numbers 11:23) "Is the Lord's arm too short?" As did the Israelites, we all too often do not give God enough credit, or even believe, that He can do His job. (Matthew 19:26) "With man this is impossible, but with God, all things are possible."

God wants us to pray for our loved ones and friends that are not saved. (I Timothy 2:1-4) "I urge, then, first of all, that requests, prayers, intercession, and thanksgiving be made for everyone--for kings and all those in authority, that we may live peaceful and quiet lives in all godliness and holiness. This is good and pleases God our Savior, who wants all men to be saved and to come to the knowledge of the truth." If we pray according to God's will, He will answer our prayers. (I John 5:14) "This is the confidence we have in approaching God: that if we ask anything according to His will, He hears us. And if we know that He hears us--whatever we ask--we know that we have what we asked of Him." God wants us to pray for the salvation of others. He does not want anyone to perish. (II Peter 3:9) "He is patient with you, not wanting anyone to perish, but everyone to come to repentance."

Praying for someone you love or know does help. God does hear those prayers and answers them. Moses prayed for the Israelites time and time again whenever they sinned against the Lord. Due to His great mercy and compassion and for the glory of His name, He forgave them. He disciplined them, but He forgave them. Just as Moses interceded for the Israelites, God will hear our heartfelt prayers for our loved ones. (Psalm 34:17-19) "The righteous cry out, and the Lord hears them; He delivers them from all their troubles. The Lord is close to the brokenhearted and saves those who are crushed in spirit. A righteous man may have many troubles, but the Lord delivers him from them all."

After the Israelites had been in exile and the walls of Jerusalem were torn down, some years later Nehemiah went before the Lord in prayer. Previously King Artaxerxes issued an order to stop any rebuilding of the wall. The wall torn down was a symbol of where the faith of the Israelites lay, broken down. This troubled Nehemiah as it troubles us to see our loved ones away from the Lord, and he prayed to God. Nehemiah was a cupbearer to the king. He knew of the order to stop rebuilding. This did not stop him from believing in God to answer his prayers, and He did.

Although Nehemiah was afraid to ask, he still trusted God and told the king of his wish to rebuild the walls of Jerusalem. God directed the heart of the king to let him go. God never does anything halfway. He not only let him go, but the king sent army officers and cavalry with him. God also directed the events that followed to protect the rebuilding due to Nehemiah's faith. (Matthew 15:28) "Woman, you have great faith! Your request is granted." Our faith and prayers can help save our loved ones. God will use others to help answer our prayers. (I Corinthians 3:6-9) "I planted the seed, Apollos watered it, but God made it grow. So neither he who plants nor he who waters is anything, but only God, who makes things grow. The man who plants and the man who waters have one purpose, and each will be rewarded according to his own labor. For we are God's fellow workers; you are God's field, God's building."

In praying for salvation for our loved ones, they must receive Jesus Christ on their own, but God will direct their steps, as He did for Nehemiah. (Proverbs 20:24) "A man's steps are directed by the Lord. How then can anyone understand his own way?" But you must believe in what you are praying for. (John 14:12-14) "I tell you the truth, anyone who has faith in Me will do what I have been doing. He will do even greater things than these because I am going to the Father. And I will do whatever you ask in My name, so that the Son may bring glory to the Father. You may ask Me for anything in My name, and I will do it." The purpose of Jesus was to set the captives free and to bring salvation to unbelievers. (Luke 4:18-19) "The Spirit of the Lord is on me because He has anointed me to preach good news to the poor. He has sent me to proclaim freedom for the prisoners and recovery of sight for the blind, to release the oppressed, to proclaim the year of the Lord's favor." As we are God's children and want us with Him, He knows that we love our family and want them with us in heaven as well. (Acts 16:31) "Believe in the Lord Jesus, and you will be saved--you and your household."

In the Book of I Samuel, the Israelites asked for a king. This did not please God. He was their King, but He gave them one anyway. He chose Saul, who was a Benjamite, to be the first king. Some people did not accept Saul. The Ammonites seized a town of Israel, Jabesh-Gilead. Word of this came to Saul and the Spirit of the Lord came over him. He burned with anger. With the help of the Lord, Saul and the warriors he gathered to fight with him conquered the Ammonites. This won the favor of the people and they confirmed him as king. Some things may look bad, but God can take a bad situation and turn it into a blessing. (Romans 8:28) "And we know that in all things God works for the good of those who love Him, who have been called according to His purpose." So in waiting on God to answer your prayers never go on what you see. (II Corinthians 4:18) "So we fix our eyes not on what is seen, but on what is unseen. For what is seen is temporary, but what is unseen is eternal."

Some things that you pray for may not be in your best interest and God may answer in a different way than you thought, or He may be telling you to wait. There are things that God can answer right away. But if it is something more involved, or spiritual with yourself or someone you love, don't give up. In Luke 18, Jesus is telling the story of a widow who kept coming to a judge to get justice against her adversary. He kept refusing. Then finally he gave in, (Luke 18:4) "Even though I don't fear God or care about men, yet because this widow keeps bothering me, I will see that she gets justice, so that she won't eventually wear me out with her coming!"

We are never to give up. Satan will try to discourage you, telling you that your prayer will never get answered. That is a lie! He is the father of lies! (John 8:44) "You belong to your father, the devil, and you want to carry out your father's desire. He was a murderer from the beginning, not holding to the truth, for there is no truth in him. When he lies, he speaks his native language, for he is a liar and the father of lies." He wants you to be discouraged and give up. So, get stubborn and don't give up. That is one thing that keeps me going through all my trials. I refuse to let Satan win or have my family! They belong to me and God! (Luke 18:7-8) "Listen to what the unjust judge says. And will not God bring about justice for His chosen ones, who cry out to Him day and night? Will He keep putting them off? I tell you, He will see that they get justice, and quickly."

You may be praying for some sort of deliverance from something terrible. It may seem to be taking forever. But, take heart. Wait on God. He will deliver you. (Psalm 27:14) "Wait for the Lord; be strong and take heart and wait on the Lord." The trials you are going through may be what the Lord is using to change some things in your heart and heal your hurts. I know this from experience. We are always learning something new and growing during our Christian walk on earth.

When I was first saved, the littlest thing that went wrong between me and my husband would hurt me deeply. As I have gone through many difficulties and hardships, I kept trusting in God and reading His Word. The more time I spent with Him, the more I changed and the stronger I got. As with anything in life that you want to complete and do your best at, you must finish the task at hand before moving on to something new. This is the way it is with the trials of life. God lets you go through trials to mold you. Some are to develop patience in you, some are to make you stronger, and some are to increase your faith. As you pass these tests you grow as a Christian. Through each trial you pass, you move on to the next step of your Christian growth and your deliverance.

Sometimes in your deliverance, God needs to work things out in you, things that you may not see at first. As you see God take you from struggle to struggle and answer your prayers along the way, getting you through each one, you see that God truly is there for you and that He loves you. This increases your faith in Him. You begin to see and know that "He will never leave you nor forsake you." This is why He lets you go through trials. He loves you and wants you to trust Him, as you do for your own children. Some things need to be learned by experience to become a part of your spirit and the way that you think. Through each trial, as you grow closer to God, and as you keep reading His Word, your mind is transformed. (Romans 12:2) "Do not conform any longer to the patterns of this world, but be transformed by the renewing of your mind."

Taking tests in school you either pass or fail. Well, good news! With God, there is no failing! You get to take the tests over and over until you pass! The sooner you learn, the sooner you get through your trial and on to your deliverance. God wants you to grow as a Christian. He wants you to pass the test! So, how you go through each trial and the attitude you go through it with determines how quickly you pass, and are delivered into the next step of your growth or delivered from the bad situation that you are in.

There is a time for everything. God has a plan and He will help you along the way. He will put people in your path to help you understand things, to comfort you, and to just be a friend in the Lord. Something we all need and need to be to one another. (Ecclesiastes 3:1-8) "There is a time for everything, and a season for every activity under heaven: a time to be born and a time to die, a time to plant and a time to uproot, a time to kill and a time to heal, a time to tear down and a time to build, a time to weep and a time to laugh, a time to mourn and a time to dance, a time to scatter stones and a time to gather them, a time to embrace and a time to refrain, a time to search and a time to give up, a time to keep and a time throw away, a time to tear and a time to mend, a time to be silent, and a time to speak, a time to love and a time to hate, a time for war and a time for peace." War or the trials you go through will help you to grow if you let God teach you as you walk through them. God will give you peace as you go through them, and not just when your prayers are answered or you are delivered. There is a time for trials, the growth process, and a time for peace or victory!

Once you pass the test of faith you will have the ability to be in the presence of God no matter where you are; where God is, peace resides.

You can be in the middle of a storm, Satan attacking you in all directions through people, finances, or your job. You can still, in all the turmoil going on all around you, be in the presence of the Almighty. You can have the peace that surpasses all understanding in the middle of your storm. Just as it was with Jesus and the disciples one day as they sailed to the other side of the lake they were on. (Luke 8:23-24) "As they sailed, He fell asleep. A squall came down on the lake so that the boat was being swamped, and they were in great danger. The disciples went and woke Him saying, 'Master, Master, we're going to drown!' He got up and rebuked the wind and the raging waters; the storm subsided, and all was calm." If you put your trust in Jesus, He will calm the storms of your life as well.

Your joy needs to come from the Lord and not from the world or the people in it. (Nehemiah 8:10) "Do not grieve, for the joy of the Lord is your strength." People will always disappoint you. God never will. He is always faithful. (Deuteronomy 7:9) "Know therefore that the Lord your God is God; He is the faithful God, keeping His covenant of love to a thousand generations of those who love Him and keep His commandments."

I have been through some rough storms. It was only when I learned through the trials, that my joy came from the Lord. You know this in your mind, but it sometimes takes a little longer for it to get through to your heart. I truly thank God for teaching me this through the trials I faced. I am a better person for it. Your Heavenly Father is the one who brings you peace. Not the world. I just want to be where He is, always. In His presence, there is peace, contentment, and joy. I have been through hurt, from the loss of my son, the loss of my mother, the problem with my husband's alcohol and drug addictions, and the pain that it caused. I have been through similar problems with my older son, and pain from my husband and son at war with each other constantly. This was happening all during the same period. I was getting attacked in all directions.

The love of God the Father was the only way I made it through those difficult times. You cannot fight a spiritual battle with Satan by yourself and win. He provided strength, comfort, and protection through Him and His Word speaking to my spirit, and friends that He placed in my path along the way to be a shoulder to cry on or an encouragement when I needed it. Through this, I learned that God supplied the needs of my son, who was in college at the time, and my husband and mine. I learned that He was always there for me, even when I threw temper tantrums from time to time and my faith took a nosedive. He always gently restored my faith and picked me back up.

Through that storm where everything was going wrong and the pain in my heart was overwhelming, I learned that God was in control. He wanted me to realize this; once I did, I realized how gentle He always was with me, even when I knew I let Him down. I found the peace and joy I needed to get through my trials until I was finally delivered, and my husband was saved.

There will always be trials of some sort for all Christians as long as you are here on earth, but I have learned who is in control and where my strength and comfort come from. I know to call on Him and He will always be faithful to pick me back up. (II Samuel 22:2-4) "The Lord is my Rock, my Fortress and my Deliverer; my God is my Rock, in whom I take refuge, my Shield and the horn of my salvation. He is my Stronghold, my Refuge, and my Savior--from violent men you save me. I call to the Lord, who is worthy of praise, and I am saved from my enemies."

Though being attacked in every direction by Satan, I learned how to be in the presence of the Almighty. It is by trusting Him, submitting to Him, obeying Him, and knowing that He truly is in control and that He loves you. (Psalm 91:1) "Trust in God and rest in the shadow of the Almighty."

12

Brotherly Love

(John 15:12-13) "My command is this: Love each other as I have loved you. Greater love has no one than this that he lay down his life for his friends." This is the greatest showing of brotherly love that there is, demonstrated by our Lord and Savior, Jesus Christ. He gave His life for all of mankind so that we might have eternal life. We as Christians are to testify of our Lord and Savior; not only in words but also in the way we live our daily lives. (II Timothy 1:8) "So do not be ashamed to testify about our Lord, or ashamed of me His prisoner."

We as Christians can lay down our lives every day in the way that we live. (I John 3:16-18) "This is how we know what love is: Jesus Christ laid down His life for us. And we ought to lay down our lives for our brothers. If anyone has material possessions and sees his brother in need but has no pity on him, how can the love of God be in him? Dear children, let us not love with words or tongue but with actions and in truth." We do this by loving our fellow man and giving when we have to give, whether it is time, a shoulder to cry on money or possessions. (Matthew 5:42) "Give to the one who asks you and does not turn away from the one who wants to borrow from you."

There are ministering angels everywhere, here on earth. They are in the form of every person who lends a helping hand or a shoulder to cry on, to comfort those in need. (Hebrews 1:14) "Are not all angels ministering spirits sent to serve those who will inherit salvation?" They are the people who are always there, to encourage you, to point you in the right direction according to God's Word, and to tell you they love you. (Hebrews 13:1-2) "Keep on loving each other as brothers. Do not forget to entertain strangers, for by so doing some people have entertained angels without knowing it."

This is another way God shows His love for us. God uses us. We are His hands and we are the voice He uses to tell His dear children that He loves them. (I John 4:7-8) "Dear friends, let us love one another, for love comes from God. Everyone who loves has been born of God and knows God. Whoever does not love does not know God, because God is love." There are helping hand centers all over the country, places that people like you and me volunteer to work at and donate to. Food, clothing, household items, and money are donated to these places to help people who have fallen on hard times. In this way, God's love is shining through them. (Galatians 6:2) "Carry each other's burdens, and in this way, you will fulfill the law of Christ."

The United States of America helps out the people of our own country with organizations such as United Way, the Red Cross, Salvation Army, Goodwill Industries, Soup Kitchens and Homeless Shelters, and even organizations to help people get a home such as Habitat for Humanity. The United States also helps out countries with starving people through donations supplied by different food companies. There are Christian organizations as well, that minister to other countries. They donate food and their time in teaching their children and adults about water irrigation etc. and especially about the love of Jesus. A lot of people get angry when they hear of all the United States does for other countries, but they shouldn't, for they are only doing the will of God. (Hebrews 6:10-11) "God is not unjust; He will not forget your work and the love you have shown Him as you have helped His people and continue to help them. We want each of you to show this same diligence to the very end, in order to make your hope sure."

In the Book of II Samuel 9:1-12, David, who is now king was looking for someone still left in Saul's family. If you remember, After he was anointed as king, Saul became jealous of David. David had a heart for God and His will. The Lord was with him. With the help of the Lord, David defeated tens of thousands of their enemies, more than Saul. The people loved him. This made Saul jealous. Saul vowed to kill David. He constantly searched after him. God always protected him. Saul and his sons were eventually killed. Though Saul continually plotted to kill David, David loved him. This showed that David truly had the love of God in him. Sometime later after being anointed as king, David searched for someone in Saul's family whom he could show kindness to. He found the son of Jonathan, Mephibosheth. Jonathan was one of Saul's sons who was killed in battle. Mephibosheth was crippled in both feet. David gave him all the property that used to belong to Saul. In addition to that, David told him that he and his sons would always eat at his table. This was a love deep from within his heart, a love from God. Mephibosheth's crippled feet symbolize our crippled state as sinners and deep heartaches before Jesus makes us whole in purifying our souls. (Exodus 15:26) "For I am the Lord, who heals you."

There have been many times that I have been down and discouraged, and the love of a friend picked me up. She would tell me a verse that I knew was from God because it would enlighten my heart and raise my spirit again. This is how we, as Christians, need to be. (I Corinthians 13:13) "And now these three remain faith, hope and love. But the greatest of these is love." As long as Satan roams the earth, he breeds doom and despair. We can counteract everything Satan does to our fellow man if more people would let God use them. We are the vessels God uses to comfort His brokenhearted children. (I Peter 1:22) "Now that you have purified yourselves by obeying the truth so that you have sincere love for your brothers, love one another deeply, from the heart."

After the death of Jesus, the apostles preached the good news of Jesus and salvation. More and more people were born into the family of God. In the Book of Acts 4:32, it says that all the believers were of one heart and mind. They all shared everything. (Hebrews 13:16) "And do not forget to do good and to share with others, for with such sacrifices God is pleased."

If we truly want the love of Jesus to shine through us, we need to show it. Actions speak louder than words. (I John 2:5-6) "This is how we know we are in Him: Whoever claims to live in Him must walk as Jesus did." We need to love all people, and share with all people when we are able to do so, not just other 'believers.'

We are to share with those who do not believe as well, this may be the only way some people might experience the love of Jesus. (Luke 6:31-32) "Do to others as you would have them do to you. If you love those who love you, what credit is that to you? Even 'sinners' love those who love them." As you do this, especially when someone who is not 'saved' and has wronged you, they will wonder why. They will wonder why you are so nice and forgiving when they haven't been to you. (Proverbs 25:21-22) "If your enemy is hungry, give him food to eat; if he is thirsty, give him water to drink. In doing this, you will heap burning coals on his head, and the Lord will reward you." This is a good way of showing your faith in Jesus. After all, we as sinners, before receiving the gift of salvation, are all enemies of God as long as we continue to live in sin; yet Jesus, though sinless Himself, died for us. So, how can we turn anyone away who is in need, when Jesus said in (Luke 22:42) "Father, if you are willing, take this cup from Me; yet not My will, but Yours be done." This may be difficult at times with some people, but if you call on the Lord to show His love for them through you, He will. (Philippians 4:13) "I can do everything through Him who gives me strength."

Do you remember the story of the Good Samaritan? It is a story of true brotherly love and hospitality. (Romans 12:13) "Share with God's people who are in need. Practice hospitality." It is found in the Book of Luke 10:30-37. The Jews, because of their different worship, despised Samaritans. The story tells of a man who was going down from Jerusalem to Jericho. On the way, someone robbed him, stripped him of his clothes, beat him, and went away. Two people passed him, a priest and a Levite. Neither bothered to stop and help the man. A Samaritan did and he bandaged his wounds, put him on his donkey, and took him to an inn and took care of him. He gave the innkeeper some money and asked him to look after the man until he returned, and if the innkeeper incurred any extra expense, he would reimburse him when he returned. The Samaritan went out of his way to help the man. He showed true love deep from within his heart. (I Peter 4:8-9) "Above all, love each other deeply, because love covers over a multitude of sins. Offer hospitality to one another without grumbling."

We are called to do the same for our fellow man. As you reach out and help someone, you are richly rewarded. You are rewarded deep within your heart. Your heart grows each time you reach out to someone out of sincere love. (I Corinthians 15:58) "Always give yourselves fully to the work of the Lord, because you know that your labor in the Lord is not in vain." It is a wonderful feeling to help someone and know that you made a difference in his or her life. There is no small gesture in love. No matter what you do, even if it is a phone call to someone to cheer them up, it is still an act of love. There are many ways you can be a 'good Samaritan.' The more you reach out to someone else, in doing so you are reaching out to God.   The 'good Samaritan' not only reached out to someone he didn't know, but it was someone whom he should have felt contempt for because he was not a brother in faith to the man. Yet he showed sincere love for him and truly helped him. Jesus did the same for us. He paid the price for our sins.

As sinners, we are all hurting. Our souls are from the sin within. Jesus heals our souls and makes us alive again! (Ephesians 2:4-5) "But because of His great love for us, God, who is rich in mercy, made us alive with Christ even when we were dead in transgressions--it is by grace you have been saved."

13

Strength

(Exodus 15:2) "The Lord is my strength and my song; He has become my salvation." There are two ways of being exhausted: there is physical exhaustion, and there is mental exhaustion. I have heard people say that mental exhaustion is just as tiring as physical labor. I know that to be true. My emotions have been in such a whirlwind with the constant pain that I have felt due to the trials and personal losses I have experienced. There are days when I am missing my son so much, and the pain is so great along with the other troubles of my life, I feel completely worn out. You don't think that you can take anything else bad happening in your life. That is where the love of God the Father comes in. He will supply you with the strength that you need to endure your trials and persevere to the end. (Psalm 73:26) "My flesh and my heart may fail, but God is the strength of my heart and my portion forever."

There have been a lot of times when I thought that I just couldn't go on. It wasn't the right time for my deliverance yet. Just as you cannot take a cake out of the oven before it is done, so it is with the trials of life. God will not put more on you than you can handle. I have found out that God knows a whole lot more than I do about what I can and cannot handle. (I Corinthians 10:12-13) "So, if you think you are standing firm, be careful that you don't fall! No temptation has seized you except what is common to man. And God is faithful; He will not let you be tempted beyond what you can bear. But when you are tempted, He will also provide a way out so that you can stand up under it."

God proved me wrong time and time again. He has provided me with the strength to continue, to persevere. God is our refuge and He wants us to run to Him when we are weary. Jesus knew what weariness was as He told the disciples that went with Him to pray in the Garden of Gethsemane the night He was betrayed; (Mark 14:34) "My soul is over-whelmed with sorrow to the point of death." Yet, as overwhelmed as He was He still prayed for the Father's will to be done and not His. (Mark 14:36) "Abba, Father, everything is possible for You. Take this cup from Me. Yet not what I will, but what You will." Just call on Him when you are weary and worn and He will give you strength. (Psalm 46:1) "God is our refuge and strength and ever-present help in times of trouble."

There are people, that as you read through the Bible, you will see how they endured their trials and struggles with God's help and protection. He was there to comfort them spiritually and give them the strength to continue to fulfill His purpose and plan for their lives. Paul is one of them. As I have said earlier, he wrote 13 of the Books in the New Testament, 5 of which were written in prison. Imagine back then what a prison cell must have looked like and the heat he had to endure, and he still did God's will. He wrote in (II Corinthians 12:9-10) "Therefore I will boast all the more gladly about my weaknesses, so that Christ's power may rest on me. That is why, for Christ's sake, I delight in weaknesses, in insults, in hardships, in persecutions, in difficulties. For when I am weak, then I am strong."

It is when you are weak due to the hardships of life that you are humbled. It is in our weaknesses that God works through us, and His glory is revealed in us as we overcome our trials. The people who know us and the hardships that we experience see us overcome our trials with victory, and the glory of God shines through us to them. Paul learned that God's strength is made perfect in him. (II Samuel 22:33) "It is God who arms me with strength and makes my way perfect."

My mother passed away on December 26, 2002, due to complications from Parkinson's disease. Parkinson's disease affects your nervous system and your muscles. The more you keep active the longer it takes for the disease to progress. My mother was always active and she hated to watch TV. She always had to be doing something. She had the disease for 22 years, the last 10 being the most difficult for her and my father, who was always there to take care of her. She had a Nordic-Track machine. With Parkinson's, she couldn't get the muscle coordination and strength to use it. But that did not stop her. She was very determined and finally succeeded. It took her 20 minutes to just be able to start moving on it. As she kept with it she got better. Her Parkinson's doctor was amazed! He had told her when she mentioned trying to start using it, that she would never do it. He was wrong; he did not know my mother. She lost weight with it and her muscle coordination improved. God gives every one of us the same determination and strength to keep going if we would only call on Him. (Philippians 4:13) "I can do everything through Him who gives me strength."

My mother also loved God very much. Over the years she had one operation or another from injuring herself. The injuries hurt her physically and she had to stay off her feet. Each time that happened, the disease progressed a little more. But she always relied on God for her strength. It never got the best of her or her spirit. She loved every one. Even at times when my other siblings or I would unintentionally hurt her feelings, she always forgave us and always tried to do everything she could for us. She always tried to make sure we had what we needed. She would go out of her way to make sure that our birthdays and Christmas were special. She loved unconditionally. That kind of love only comes from God.

God gave her strength to endure and kept her spirit high, even when it got to the point where she was in a wheelchair most of the time. She loved sewing and making different kinds of craft projects. She also loved plants and flowers. She would wheel herself out to the yard and from her wheelchair would water and take care of her plants. They were always beautiful. She had a green thumb. She used to be a Trust Officer at a bank when she was diagnosed with Parkinson's disease. She kept working until the disease got too much for her. She had an important job and an active life. Most people would get depressed when going from the lifestyle she had to knowing that you would end up in a wheelchair, depending on someone else to take care of you. God's love kept her strong and it kept her going.

I miss her very much, but now she is walking and running alongside her Heavenly Father! (Isaiah 40:28-31) "Do you not know? Have you not heard? The Lord is the everlasting God, the Creator of the ends of the earth. He will not grow tired or weary, and His understanding no one can fathom. He gives strength to the weary and increases the power of the weak. Even youths grow tired and weary and young men stumble and fall, but those who hope in the Lord will renew their strength. They will soar on wings like eagles; they will run and not grow weary, they will walk and not grow faint."

If you read the story of Joseph in the Book of Genesis, you will find that God was with him as well; his father, Jacob, favored him. His brothers were jealous of him. They sold him into slavery, and later he was put into prison before becoming the head of Egypt. God was with him the whole time. Joseph trusted God and submitted to His will. The Lord stayed with him, protected him, and gave him the strength to endure until the Lord directed his path to the favor of Pharaoh. (Psalm 28:7) "The Lord is my strength and my shield; my heart trusts in Him, and I am helped."

The Lord also gives you physical strength as well when you need it. In the Book of Judges, chapter 13 is the story of Samson. He took a Nazarite vow. A Nazarite is someone who is set apart from birth. At the time of conception, the mother is to drink no alcohol or eat anything unclean. He is to use no razor on his head or face. Samson was to be a Nazarite from birth to death. The Spirit of the Lord was with him and made him very strong.

In the Book of I Kings during the reign of Ahab, king of Israel, there had been a drought for a few years. God told Elijah, the prophet, to tell Ahab that the Lord was going to send rain, and for him to assemble all the people. God wanted to show the people and their false prophets, who were worshiping Baal, that He was the only true God. King Ahab's wife,

Jezebel, was killing God's prophets. This was the reason for the drought and why He was now sending rain. God told Elijah to get two bulls, cut them into pieces, and put them on separate piles of wood. Their false prophets were to call to their god, to bring fire down on the wood and the bull, and Elijah was to do the same. Their god did nothing, but when Elijah called to the God in heaven, God brought fire down from heaven and consumed the bull. Then as God had directed, Elijah killed all of the false prophets.

King Ahab told his wife all that Elijah had done. She wanted to kill Elijah. After all, God had done through him, you would not expect him to be scared of her, but he was and he ran for fear of his life to Horeb. He came to a broom tree. Tired from his journey, he laid down to sleep. An angel of the Lord got him up two times to feed him and give him something to drink to strengthen him again. Even though he ran in fear, God still protected him and strengthened him. (Isaiah 41:10) "So do not fear, for I am with you; do not be dismayed, for I am your God. I will strengthen you and help you; I will uphold you with My righteous right hand."

David is another one who received God's protection, comfort, and strength. He kept running from King Saul, who was hunting him down to kill him out of jealousy as well, though he did nothing wrong. He still trusted in God. God gave him strength to endure and protected him until He finally delivered him from his troubles and was anointed as the second king to rule over Israel.

Just as God gave these people strength to endure their trials until they reached the purpose and plans He had for them, He will do the same for you and me. In order that we might become the people that God wants us to be, we need to go through our trials and persevere to the end until we reach the other side, our deliverance. The trials change us, but God is the one who keeps us strong. He comforts you when you are down and is always faithful to you and your burdens. He loves you unconditionally. He has a better place planned for all of us who receive His Son, Jesus Christ. The only true King of Kings. (Psalm 29:11) "The Lord gives strength to His people; the Lord blesses His people with peace." Through the rocky roads of life, you cannot make it and overcome without Jesus in your heart. But with Him, you can endure everything. You can overcome and see the deliverance and answer to your prayers. He gives you all the strength you need to persevere to the end. (I Corinthians 1:8-9) "He will keep you strong to the end so that you will be blameless on the day of our Lord Jesus Christ. God, who has called you into fellowship with his Son Jesus Christ our Lord, is faithful." Glory be to God!

14

Victory

Victory is after living in habitual sin, being able to be cleansed and purified from them. Victory is in knowing that now you are eternally saved, when once you were doomed to an eternity in hell. (I Corinthians 15:54-57) "Death has been swallowed up in victory. Where, O death, is your victory? Where, O death, is your sting? The sting of death is sin, and the power of sin is the law. But thanks be to God! He gives us the victory through our Lord Jesus Christ." Victory over sin and victory passing through our trials, and in our answered prayers is another way God shows His love for us.

In the Book of Deuteronomy, God says to the Israelites as they cross over to the Promised Land that they are not to be afraid, that He will be with them and they will be victorious. They will be victorious as long as they love the Lord their God with all their hearts, and trust and obey Him. But if they do not obey Him, they will surely die in battle. God tells us how to gain victory over our enemies. We are to trust and obey Him, and He will go with us through our trials and deliver victory into our hands. (Deuteronomy 20:3-4) "Hear, O Israel, today you are going into battle against your enemies. Do not be fainthearted or afraid; do not be terrified or give way to panic before them. For the Lord your God is the One who goes with you to fight for you against your enemies to give you victory."

The enemies that we face are the day-to-day trials that we go through, whether it is a job, financial difficulties, trouble with someone you love, or you are praying for a lost loved one. God says if you submit to His will if you love, trust, and obey Him, you will have victory! (Psalm 60:12) "With God we will gain the victory, and He will trample down our enemies."

In the Book of Joshua, the Israelites are about to take over the city of Jericho. The Lord tells Joshua to have armed men march around the city once for six days. Seven priests were to carry trumpets of rams' horns in front of the ark. On the seventh day, they were to march around the city seven times with the priests blowing the trumpets. When the people heard the trumpets, they were to give a shout and the wall of the city would collapse and every man was to go straight in and take it over. God gave them specific instructions and as long as they followed it, He would deliver the city into their hands. (Isaiah 43:13) "No one can deliver out of My hand. When I act, who can reverse it?" Isn't that awesome? No matter what you are up against, if you obey and trust God, the outcome of your problem will be a victory!

Jericho and its walls around it were very strong, just like a heart that had been hardened by sin. Nothing is too difficult for the Lord; even the hardest of hearts. (Jeremiah 32:27) "I am the Lord, the God of all mankind. Is anything too hard for Me?" The walls tumbling down symbolize a heart hardened by sin, and melting when receiving forgiveness of sin in coming to Jesus Christ. (Ezekiel 36:26) "I will give you a new heart and put a new spirit in you; I will remove from you your heart of stone and give you a heart of flesh." The trumpet blasts and shouts are the heartfelt prayers of God's children. (Proverbs 15:29) "The Lord is far from the wicked but He hears the prayer of the righteous."

Victory is finally being delivered from your trials. Just as in the story of Joseph when after years of separation from his family, slavery, and imprisonment, he was finally reunited with his brothers and his father. Victory is in the story of Hannah in the Book of I Samuel. After years of being married and conceiving no children, she prayed, fasted, and wept bitterly before the Lord for a child. The Lord heard her prayer, and she conceived a child. Victory is in the story of Daniel and the lion's den. Daniel's enemies plotted for a way to have him thrown into the lion's den and found it. He was thrown into the lion's den and when the king came to see if he had been harmed the next morning, he was completely safe. There was not a scar on him or one hair on his head harmed. The Lord protected him and gave him victory over his enemies.

Victory is also the Israelites finally crossing over into the Promised Land after forty years of wandering in the desert. Satan will always try to thwart the plans of God. But with God, he will always lose. He may temporarily halt the success of God's plans due to disobedience on our part, or fear and panic seem to overwhelm us. The Israelites were disobedient to God. They started worshipping other gods and making idols for themselves. This temporary delay was the fault of the Israelites and not God. God is always faithful to us. (Deuteronomy 7:9) "Know therefore that the Lord your God is God; He is the faithful God, keeping His covenant of love to a thousand generations of those who love Him and keep His commands." He doesn't move; we do. You reap what you sow. There are consequences for every action. If you are doing something wrong and are disciplined by God for it, do not blame Him because of something you are doing wrong. Just as you discipline your children and are just in doing so, so is the Lord your God. (Proverbs 3:11-12) "My son, do not despise the Lord's discipline and do not resent His rebuke, because the Lord disciplines those He loves, as a father the son He delights in."

An idol is, according to Webster's New American Dictionary, "an image of a god, used as an object of worship or an object of ardent or excessive devotion." According to the words of this dictionary, an idol is something that you worship and anything that you worship is your lord or master. (Dictionary, 1995) (II Peter 2:19) "For a man is a slave to whatever has mastered him." There should be only one who is the master over you, and that is the Lord your God. (Exodus 20:3) "You shall have no other gods before me." What kind of idols do you have in your life? What kinds of addictions have mastered you? Are you truly worshipping the Lord your God as you should? (II Peter 3:11-12) "You ought to live holy and godly lives as you look forward to the day of God and speed its coming." Just as the Israelites were delayed due to their disobedience, your victory may be delayed for the same reason, although that is not always the case. Examine your heart and soul and see how much of the delay that you may be experiencing is your own fault and stop blaming God.

Delayed victory over a trial you are going through or an answer to a prayer may also be a spiritual battle and not something that you have done. In the Book of Daniel, Daniel is given a vision from the Lord and it troubled him greatly. He did not understand it and went before the Lord in prayer. He prayed for God to turn His wrath away from Jerusalem and His holy hill and forgive the sins of the people for His namesake.

The understanding of the vision came later, and an angel explained the delay. (Daniel 10:11-14) "Daniel, you who are highly esteemed, consider carefully the words I am about to speak to you and stand up, for I have now been sent to you.' And when he said this to me, I stood up trembling. Then he continued, 'Do not be afraid, Daniel. Since the first day that you set your mind to gain understanding and to humble yourself before your God, your words were heard, and I have come in response to them. But the prince of the Persian kingdom resisted me for twenty-one days. Then Michael, one of the chief princes, came to help me because I was detained there with the king of Persia. Now I have come to explain to you what will happen to your people in the future, for the vision concerns a time yet to come."

The prince of the Persian kingdom the scripture is talking about here, is a supernatural creature who tried to direct the human rulers of Persia to oppose God's plan. There are evil angels that seek to influence the affairs of nations and God's people. Due to this, we are never to give up praying and never give up on God. (Luke 18:1) "Then Jesus told His disciples a parable to show them that they should always pray and not give up." If you keep on praying and submitting to God's will, you will see the answer to your prayers and victory over your trials. Satan may try, but he will never succeed against the Lord. (Proverbs 21:30-31) "There is no wisdom, no insight, no plan that can succeed against the Lord. The horse is made ready for the day of battle, but victory rests with the Lord." Trust in God to give you the victory over the trials that you are facing and never doubt God's almighty power, love, and strength. (Job 11:7-9) "Can you fathom the mysteries of God? Can you probe the limits of the Almighty? They are higher than the heavens--what can you do? They are deeper than the depths of the grave--what can you know? Their measure is longer than the earth and wider than the sea."

During the reign of Jotham king of Judah and Jeroboam king of Israel, the Reubenites, Gadites, and half-tribe of Manasseh, waged war against the Hagrites, Jetur, Naphish, and Nodab. They cried out to the Lord in prayer to give them victory. Due to their trust in God, He gave them the victory. (Psalm 44:6-8) "I do not trust in my bow, my sword does not bring me victory, but You give us victory over our enemies, You put our adversaries to shame. In God, we make our boast all day long, and we will praise Your name forever."

Your Almighty Father in Heaven has proved time and time again to His faithful servants that He was with them, protected them from their enemy, and delivered victory into their hands. He did this with Elisha and Israel in the Book of II Kings. The king of Aram was at war with Israel and through the Word of the Lord, Elisha warned Israel each time the army of Aram set out to attack Israel. Aram sent out horses and chariots in strong forces to capture Elisha when they heard that he was the one warning Israel. Elisha's servant became frightened. The forces that are against us are just as strong and powerful, but God is stronger. Elisha trusted God and knew that God was stronger than any force or army of Aram. (Psalm 44:3) "It was not by their sword that they won the land, nor did their arm bring them victory; it was Your right hand, Your arm, and the light of Your face, for You loved them." Elisha told his servant not to be afraid, that there was more with them than with the enemy. (Romans 8:31) "What, then, shall we say in response to this? If God is for us, who can be against us?"

To all of you who are praying for a lost loved one or friend, there is victory in seeing them finally receive forgiveness for their sins and accept

Jesus Christ into their hearts! Praying for a lost soul and finally seeing them receive Jesus Christ and know that they are eternally saved is more rewarding than anything else in the world. There is no greater joy, no greater beauty than to see a soul washed in the blood of our Savior Jesus Christ! (Psalm 118:14-15) "The Lord is my strength and my song; He has become my salvation. Shouts of joy and victory resound in the tents of the righteous: The Lord's right hand has done mighty things!"

There is nothing that can defeat a child of God. Nothing can separate you from His love and protection. There is nothing that can stand up against God and win. Jesus Christ defeated sin for us. He has already won the victory for us. We just need to accept His free gift. Through the work of the Holy Spirit within your heart, He will guide you on your journey through life's rocky roads. To help us grow as Christians we must go through trials, but God loved us so much, that He told us the outcome in advance! We win! Trust in His promises and not in what you see. (II Corinthians 4:18) "So we fix our eyes not on what is seen, but on what is unseen. For what is seen is temporary, but what is unseen is eternal." You just need to submit and receive His forgiveness and know that God loves you, and nothing can take that away from you. The victory is yours. (Romans 8:35-39) "Who shall separate us from the love of Christ? Shall trouble or hardship or persecution or famine or nakedness or danger or sword? As it is written: 'For your sake, we face death all day long; we are considered a sheep to be slaughtered.' No, in all these things we are more than conquerors through Him who loved us. For I am convinced that neither death nor life, neither angels nor demons, neither the present nor the future, nor any powers, neither height nor depth nor anything else in all creation will be able to separate us from the love of God that is in Christ Jesus our Lord."

15

Forgiveness

(Luke 23:34) "Father, forgive them, for they do not know what they are doing." In traveling down life's highway to the road of forgiveness, the road is full of heartache and many hardships and difficulties. It is full of sin and rebellion as long as you have not received Jesus Christ into your heart. The weight of the oppression from the sin you are living in is very heavy. You feel like you live day to day with a ton of bricks on your shoulders and heart. I have felt that weight and it is impossible to get rid of it in any way other than by admitting that you are a sinner, asking forgiveness of your sins, and receiving Jesus Christ into your heart. (Romans 3:23-25) "For all have sinned and fall short of the glory of God, and are justified freely by His grace through the redemption that came by Christ Jesus. God presented Him as a sacrifice of atonement, through faith in His blood."

As soon as you admit your sins and ask forgiveness, the weight is lifted and you feel as light as a feather and just as free! This is another showing of God's awesome love for us and something that we cannot live without. (Psalm 103:11-12) "For as high as the heavens are above the earth, so great is His love for those who fear Him; as far as the east is from the west, so far has He removed our transgressions from us."

When you become a Christian, this does not mean that you are then perfect and are armed with an immunity to sin. As long as you are still human and made of flesh, you will make mistakes and sin from time to time, for we all 'fall short' and God knows this. (Ecclesiastes 7:20) "There is not a righteous man on earth who does what is right and never sins." But you no longer live in the state of continued habitual sin, and without care in doing so. As one of God's children, He will convict you by the power of the Holy Spirit and let you know when you have done wrong. (John 16:8) "When He comes, He will convict the world of guilt in regard to sin and righteousness and judgment." When you do wrong He will discipline you, but He is faithful to forgive because as any father, He loves you. (I John 1:8-9) "If we claim to be without sin, we deceive ourselves and the truth is not in us. If we confess our sins, He is faithful and just and will forgive us our sins and purify us from all unrighteousness."

The Lord knows that we will sin from time to time because the flesh is weak, but we are to try to be perfect. (Matthew 5:48) "Be perfect, therefore, as your Heavenly Father is perfect." When you leave your old life of sin, you are to leave it completely behind.   The Israelites, as in the Book of Numbers 19, had to be purified whenever they touched anything that was considered unclean, such as a dead body.

In the Book of Deuteronomy, when the Israelites were getting ready to enter into the Promised Land, the Lord instructed them to destroy all their enemies and all idols. This is how it is with us when we receive forgiveness for our sins, in coming to our 'promised land,' which is our eternal salvation. We must leave our old life of sin behind. The enemies that we fight in a life of sin are addictions, hatred, selfishness, sexual immorality, etc. (Galatians 5:19-21) "The acts of the sinful nature are obvious: sexual immorality, impurity, and debauchery; idolatry and witchcraft; hatred, discord, jealousy, fits of rage, selfish ambition, dissensions, factions, and envy; drunkenness, orgies, and the like. I warn you, as I did before, that those who live like this will not inherit the kingdom of God." When you leave your life of sin behind, your heart feels brand new. It is a wonderful feeling! (Acts 3:19-20) "Repent, then, and turn to God, so that your sins may be wiped out, that time of refreshing may come from the Lord, and that He may send the Christ, who has been appointed for you--even Jesus."

Since I have received Jesus as my personal Lord and Savior, I have learned through the day-to-day trials and experiences of life how peaceful and freeing it feels to be in the presence of the Almighty. You grow in your faith as you read the Word. Reading the Word helps you to learn the promises of God and His will for your life. You read of how through every sort of battle that His people have been through, as long as they loved, trusted, and obeyed God, He was always with them and always forgave them. When you receive Jesus, you are a new creation in Christ. (II Corinthians 5:17) "Therefore, if anyone is in Christ, He is a new creation." You have His Holy Spirit within you, but your mind is still the same. It is your heart that has changed. Your mind needs to be renewed day by day. (Ephesians 4:22-24) "You were taught, with regard to your former way of life, to put off your old self, which is being corrupted by its deceitful desires; to be made new in the attitude of your minds; and to put on the new self, created to be like God in true righteousness and holiness."

You renew your mind by spending time with God. You spend time with God by reading the Bible and in prayer, not just asking for something, but praising Him and just talking to Him. No one likes a one-sided relationship in which they are the only one who is giving. Your Heavenly Father is no different.   You also spend time with Him in reading His Word, going to church to worship Him, and fellowship with other believers as we are all called to do. (Exodus 20:8-10) "Remember the Sabbath day by keeping it holy. Six days you shall labor and do all your work, but the seventh day is a Sabbath to the Lord your God." (Matthew 4:10) "For it is written: 'Worship the Lord your God, and serve Him only." (Hebrews 10:25) "Let us not give up meeting together, as some are in the habit of doing, but let us encourage one another-- and all the more as you see the Day approaching."

The Israelites celebrated a Day of Atonement on the tenth day of the seventh month, (for them it is the month of Tishri, which is September-October for us). It was a day to be observed by the whole community to cleanse them of all their sins. They would make the proper sin offerings according to the Law. Through the sacrifice of Jesus Christ, all we have to do is go to the Lord in prayer and ask His forgiveness. (Acts 13:38-39) "Therefore, my brothers, I want you to know that through Jesus the forgiveness of sins is proclaimed to you. Through Him everyone who believes is justified from everything you could not be justified from by the Law of Moses."

The Lord your God has great mercy, compassion, and love for us all. He will forgive your sins and remember them no more. There is only one sin that He will not forgive, and that is blaspheming the Holy Spirit. (Matthew 12:31) "And so I tell you, every sin and blasphemy will be forgiven men, but the blasphemy against the Spirit will not be forgiven." Paul persecuted Christians, and upon his repentance, the Lord forgave him and used him greatly. He wrote 13 of the 27 Books of the New Testament, 5 of which were written from prison.

God forgave the Israelites over and over. Peter denied Jesus three times, and the Lord forgave him and greatly used him as well. He used him in bringing salvation to the Gentiles. The Lord showed him in Acts 10:9-16, in a vision using animals that were considered unclean to the Jewish people by Mosaic Law, that nothing or no one is unclean that God makes pure or clean. He forgives us and remembers our sins no more, they are gone and never to be used against us again. Isn't that truly amazing? We, as brothers and sisters in Christ, need to be the same way with our fellow man. (Isaiah 43:25) "I, even I, am he who blots out your transgressions, for My own sake and remembers your sins no more." He does this because He loves us, wants to bless us, and wants us with Him through all eternity.

"Blessed are they whose transgressions are forgiven, whose sins are covered. Blessed is the man whose sin the Lord will never count against him." (Romans 4:7-8)

Our Lord and Savior, Jesus Christ is our example. He set the example for us in how we are to live and treat our fellow man. What gives us the right to accept forgiveness for our sins, in which Jesus paid the price for us, and then hold a grudge against our fellow man?

"I have set you an example that you should do as I have done for you. I tell you the truth, no servant is greater than his master, nor is a messenger greater than the one who sent him. Now that you know these things, you will be blessed if you do them." (John 13:15-17)

The only thing that bitterness and unforgiveness do is hurt you. "Hatred stirs up dissension, but love covers over all wrongs." (Proverbs 10:12)

We are commanded to forgive as God forgives us; if you don't you are committing a sin and hurting your relationship with God. This is something that, with all the evil in the world, and with knowing that only God knows the day and time of our death (it can be any time,) I don't think anyone would want to take a chance on.

"All the days ordained for me were written in Your book before one of them came to be." (Psalm 139:16)

In not forgiving and holding onto bitter feelings towards someone, you are taking a chance on an eternity in hell. Not only that, but it brings a heaviness of heart that you cannot get rid of until you forgive.

"For if you forgive men when they sin against you, your Heavenly Father will also forgive you. But if you do not forgive men their sins, your Father will not forgive your sins." (Matthew 6:14-15)

It is very hard to 'turn the other cheek,' when someone has hurt you, but that is what we are called to do. "But I tell you, do not resist an evil person. If someone strikes you on the right cheek, turn to him the other also." (Matthew 5:39)

There are many people in the world today who are not saved, which makes me very sad. They are either rebelling, running from God or just don't care. Satan blinds their minds and eyes and doing the will of God does not appeal to them.

"The god of this age has blinded the minds of unbelievers so that they cannot see the light of the gospel of the glory of Christ, who is the image of God." (II Corinthians 4:4)

Only God can take the blinders off. "I, the Lord, have called you in righteousness; I will take hold of your hand. I will keep you and will make you to be a covenant for the people and a light for the Gentiles, to open eyes that are blind, to free captives from prison, and to release from the dungeon those who sit in darkness." (Isaiah 42:6-7)

Our continued attitude of love, the same love that God shows us, will eventually make them stop and think, "Why are they always so kind when I am mean to them? What is it that keeps them so loving and kind?"

"Do not repay anyone evil for evil. Be careful to do what is right in the eyes of everybody. If it is possible, as far as it depends on you, live at peace with everyone. Do not take revenge, my friends, but leave room for God's wrath, for it is written: 'It is Mine to avenge; I will repay,' says the Lord. On the contrary: If your enemy is hungry, feed him; if he is thirsty, give him something to drink. In doing this, you will heap burning coals on his head. Do not be overcome by evil, but overcome evil with good." (Romans 12:17-21)

We were enemies of Jesus while we lived in a life of sin before receiving His forgiveness, and He died for us. Out of His great love for us He forgives us; so forgive one another. Never forget what Jesus did for you.

"Praise the Lord, O my soul, and forget not all His benefits--who forgives all your sins and heals all your diseases, who redeems your life from the pit and crowns you with good things so that your youth is renewed like the eagle's." (Psalm 103:2-5)

I love the story of Joseph, Jacob's son, because in the hurt and pain, he must have felt when his brothers sold him into slavery, leading him to imprisonment, he trusted God through it all. He not only trusted God, but he showed the love of God towards his brothers when Pharaoh put him in charge of Egypt during the years of plenty and of famine. He could have been bitter and would have missed out on being a blessing to his family. The love of God showed through as he provided for his family and was reunited with them. Just as he did, we are to speak and act as Christians, showing the love of God in us at all times, for God always sees.

"Speak and act as those who are going to be judged by the law that gives freedom, because judgment without mercy will be shown to anyone who has not been merciful. Mercy triumphs over judgment." (James 2:12-13)

God sees everything, and nothing is hidden from His eyes. "The eyes of the Lord are everywhere, keeping watch on the wicked and the good." (Proverbs 15:3)

Here is a little something to think of that might help you to remember these verses:

REFLECTIONS

If Jesus were a guest in your house, would you say what you are saying? Would you do what you are doing?

Would your service to Him be pleasing? Guess what? He already is. Is He pleased?

"For a man's ways are in full view of the Lord, and He examines all his paths." (Proverbs 5:21)

Even though we are not perfect, and we make mistakes, there is comfort in knowing the abundance of God's love and forgiveness. God is always waiting and ready to forgive us.

"For I will forgive their wickedness and will remember their sins no more." (Hebrews 8:12)

Everything that we do in life apart from God (as sinners), upon asking for forgiveness, our sins are wiped out! That is an awesome show of love, mercy, and compassion! For great is God's love and mercy towards us! In the Book of II Kings, Naaman, commander of the king of Aram's army had leprosy. He went to Elisha to heal him and Elisha told him to go and wash himself in the Jordan River seven times. Naaman went away angry, he assumed that Elisha would do something great. He almost missed out on his healing. His servant asked him if he had told him to do something great, would he not have done it so, why not this?

Naaman humbled himself and did as Elisha had told him. He was cured and was very grateful! Not just for the healing, but more for the mercy that was shown. He had gone away with an attitude, but when he humbled himself and did as he was told, he was still healed. The leprosy here is a symbol of sin. The way he was healed, just by washing himself in the Jordan seven times, and how easy it was, is a symbol of how easy it is to receive forgiveness of your sins and to be saved. The washing in the Jordan is a symbol of how we are cleansed by the blood of Jesus and our sins are forgiven. Jesus is our 'living water.'

"If anyone is thirsty, let him come to Me and drink. Whoever believes in Me, as the Scripture has said, streams of living water will flow from within him." (John 7:38)

No one should ever doubt God's love. Satan tries to keep our eyes on our circumstances and make us doubt. But always remember how He made it possible to forgive you and how easy He makes it to receive. We are the ones who make it hard.

"Therefore, as God's chosen people, holy and dearly loved, clothe yourselves with compassion, kindness, humility, gentleness, and patience. Bear with each other and forgive whatever grievances you may have against one another. Forgive as the Lord forgave you. And over all these virtues put on love, which binds them all together in perfect unity." (Colossians 3:12-14)

For that is what forgiveness is all about; Love.

16

∽

Calvary

"Greater love has no one than this that he lay down his life for his friends." (John 15:13)

Our Heavenly Father has so much love for us, knowing we could never atone for all our sins on our own, He sent His One and Only Son to be that atonement for us.

"He saw that there was no one, He was appalled that there was no one to intervene; so His own arm worked salvation for Him, and His own righteousness sustained Him. He put on the righteousness as His breastplate, and the helmet of salvation on His head; He put on the garments of vengeance and wrapped Himself in zeal as in a cloak." (Isaiah 59:16-17)

This is the greatest showing of God's abundant love for us that He has; Calvary is all about love. It is where we see who we are and what we have done and nail it to the cross. It is where we can start over. It is the love of God the Father for us, so great, that He sacrificed His One and Only Son, Jesus Christ, in order that we might be saved from sin and an eternity in hell.

"I will ransom them from the power of the grave; I will redeem them from death. Where, O death, are your plagues? Where, O grave, is your destruction?" (Hosea 13:14)

When the Israelites were in bondage to the Egyptians, God sent Moses to deliver them. Pharaoh's heart was hardened, and no matter how many miracles or plagues the Lord performed through Moses, he would not let the Israelites go free. Finally, the last plague, the plague of death was set before Pharaoh. At midnight, the night of the first Passover, the Lord went throughout Egypt and every first-born male was killed. It took the death of his son to break Pharaoh's heart and finally set them free. The Israelites were to smear the top and the sides of the doorframes to their houses with the blood of a year-old lamb, a lamb without defect. The lamb symbolized Jesus Christ, who was without sin, without defect.

"God made Him who had no sin to be sin for us. So that in Him we might become the righteousness of God." (II Corinthians 5:21)

As Jesus Christ saves us from eternal damnation, the blood of the lamb over their doors protected the Israelites from death as well.

"Our God is a God who saves; from the Sovereign Lord comes escape from death." (Psalm 68:20)

In doing this, the Lord provided an escape for His people. Our Almighty Father in heaven is always in control and His plans cannot be defeated. "I know that You can do all things; no plan of Yours can be thwarted." (Job 42:2)

God is our refuge and our strength. If you place your trust and love in Him, He will always be there to protect you and to be your refuge. "Trust in the Lord at all times, O people. Pour out your hearts to Him, for God is our refuge." (Psalm 62:8)

Where is your refuge? In whom do you place your trust? You will find in life that only Jesus Christ is our one true Refuge, the only one we can count on. Man will always disappoint you, due to our natural state, we are weak. "The Lord is with me; I will not be afraid. What can man do to me?" (Psalm 118:6)

We all have human emotions sand fall to Satan's attacks at one time or another. Jesus never fell for Satan's temptations. He knew what He was sent here to do, and nothing Satan could offer Him could ever compare to the love of God, the Father.

"For the Father loves the Son and shows Him all He does. Yes, to your amazement He will show Him even greater things than these. For just as the Father raises the dead and gives them life, even so, the Son gives life to whom He is pleased to give it." (John 5:20-21)

Jesus shared in our humanity, so He understands the emotions and fears that we have and can help and protect us.

"For this reason, He had to be made like His brothers in every way, in order that He might become a merciful and faithful High Priest in service to God, and that He might make atonement for the sins of the people. Because He Himself suffered when He was tempted, He is able to help those who are being tempted." (Hebrews 2:17-18)

He shared in our humanity and felt the overwhelming weight of what He was about to undertake the night He was betrayed. But out of His great love and mercy for us, and for the love of the Father, He willingly offered Himself up for us.

"The reason My Father loves Me is that I lay down My life--only to take it up again. No one takes it from Me, but I lay it down of My own accord. I have the authority to take it up again. This command I received from My Father." (John 10:17-18)

I have found through everything I have been through, through all the rough roads with my husband and the heartaches and grief through the loss of my son and my mother, when I placed my trust in God, He led me through it all. I found peace and contentment in His presence. Every time I would get wrapped up in the circumstances that I was going through, fear and doubt would set in, and so would depression. It was only when I placed my trust in God, when I put my eyes back on Jesus, that I found peace.

"The Lord gives strength to His people; the Lord blesses His people with peace." (Psalm 29:11) You do have to do something, you have to choose to trust the Lord, you have to choose to have faith in Jesus and believe in what Calvary stands for; it stands for love and forgiveness.

"Dear friends, let us love one another, for love comes from God. This is how God showed His love among us: He sent His One and Only Son into the world so that we might live through Him. This is love: not that we loved God, but that He loved us and sent His Son as an atoning sacrifice for our sins." (I John 4:7 & 9-10)

Just as Calvary is the place where our sins are atoned for, the Israelites, at Mount Sinai, received the Ten Commandments and instructions on how to build the Tabernacle and the Ark. The Tabernacle is the place where God dwells, His sanctuary. Through the death of Jesus Christ our Lord, after receiving forgiveness of your sins, and accepting Him, He resides within your heart. Within the Tabernacle was the Most Holy Place, in which only the high priest could enter and only with a blood sacrifice, a sin offering.

"Unlike the other high priests, He does not need to offer sacrifices day after day, first for His own sins and then for the sins of the people. He sacrificed for their sins once for all when He offered Himself." (Hebrews 7:27)

The blood sacrifice represents Jesus, showing the only way to God, is through Jesus Christ. The Ark was a chest in which the Law was kept. Upon receiving Jesus into your heart, the Law is kept within your heart. Out of your love and obedience to God, you want to please Him and obey His commands. He convicts you, through the power of the Holy Spirit when you do something wrong. In your heart, you know when you are sinning against the Lord.

The Ark had a Mercy Seat or Atonement Cover, which was not only a lid for the Ark, but it was the place where sins were covered; Jesus. This also represents Calvary. Calvary is where Jesus Christ died so that we would have forgiveness of our sins, thus covering over all our sins. The curtains or veil to the Tabernacle were torn when Jesus died. This also represents Jesus. The tearing of the curtains or veil shows that now there is an opening or a way to God. That way is Jesus Christ.

In the Book of Leviticus, it describes how the Israelites had to make atonement for their sins. They had to make burnt or sin offerings to the Lord. It had to be a young male lamb without defect, just as Jesus was without sin. This never truly kept them from continuing in their sin. These kinds of offerings were done over and over. The offering that Jesus made for us was once and for all. Through His death, the Holy Spirit was made possible for us to receive. The Holy Spirit guides you through life and convicts you when you do wrong, so you are no longer living in a state of continued, habitual sin.

"I have been crucified with Christ and I no longer live, but Christ lives in me. The life I live in the body, I live by faith in the Son of God, who loved me and gave Himself for me." (Galatians 2:20)

For purification from sin, the Israelites had to take a red heifer without defect and had never been under a yoke, symbolizing never falling into the yoke of sin and the oppression it brings. They had to slaughter it outside the camp and burn it, its hide, flesh, and offal. This is also a symbol of Jesus. He was crucified outside the city. He was pure, and holy and had never sinned (under a yoke). Through receiving Him, we are purified from sin and washed clean. The man who burned the heifer had to be washed clean afterward. This also represents how we are washed clean of our sins through the blood of Jesus and how we are baptized with water as a pledge of our faith and devotion to God.

As Jesus suffered and died on the cross, we must die to our sinful nature. We must die to ourselves, take up our cross daily, and follow Him. "Wake up, O sleeper, rise from the dead and Christ will shine on you." (Ephesians 5:14)

With Jesus, we can be victorious over any persecution we may suffer from, apart from Him you have no chance at all. "For the Lord your God is the One who goes with you to fight for you against your enemies to give you victory." (Deuteronomy 20:4)

With Jesus Christ as our Lord and Savior, we will be able to live a life of love. "Be imitators of God, therefore, as dearly loved children and live a life of love, just as Christ loved us and gave Himself up for us as a fragrant offering and sacrifice to God." (Ephesians 5:1-2)

Living apart from God is a life full of pain and suffering in which there is no healing. Only God can heal a hurting heart and soul and make it whole. If you have never made Jesus the Lord of your life, read the words of this poem and ask yourself these questions.

Jonah Complex

Why do you run from Me? The
nails that were placed in My hands were for you.
The nails that were placed in My feet were for you.
The crown of thorns I wore on My head was for you.

Why do you run from Me? The
marks on My back from the beatings
I took were for you.

Why do you run from Me?
When the blood that ran down My face was for you.

Why do you run from Me?
When the blood that I shed was for you.

Why do you turn Me away and run from Me?
When I took your pain and I shed the blood
and I took your punishment.

Why do you run from Me?
I offer this for free. Yet, you still run from Me.

When you ask yourself these questions you can picture Him on the cross, dying for you and me and the whole wide world.

"But if anybody does sin, we have One who speaks to the Father in our defense--Jesus Christ, the Righteous One. He is the atoning sacrifice for our sins, and not only for ours but also for the sins of the whole world." (I John 2:1-2)

He did that so that our sins would be forgiven. How many people do you know that would die for you? Who would go to jail in place of you, and be sentenced to death in place of you? He suffered and died for our sins; yours, the whole world, and mine. He was wounded for our healing.

"But He was pierced for our transgressions, He was crushed for our iniquities; the punishment that brought us peace was upon Him, and by His wounds we are healed. We all, like sheep led astray, each of us has turned to his own way; and the Lord has laid on Him the iniquity of us all." (Isaiah 53:5-6)

"After the suffering of His soul, He will see the light of life and be satisfied; by His knowledge, My Righteous servant will justify many, and He will bear their iniquities. Therefore I will give Him a portion among the great, and He will divide the spoils with the strong, because He poured out His life unto death, and was numbered with the transgressors. For He bore the sin of many and made intercession for the transgressors." (Isaiah 53:11-12)

As Jesus hung on the cross, His last words were, (John 19:28-30) "Later, knowing that all was now completed, and so that the Scripture would be fulfilled, Jesus said, 'I am thirsty.' A jar of wine vinegar was there, so they soaked a sponge in it, put the sponge on a stalk of the hyssop plant, and lifted it to Jesus' lips. When He had received the drink, Jesus said, 'It is finished.' With that, He bowed His head and gave up His Spirit."

He loved us and even though the emotions that He Himself felt in the Garden of Gethsemane, still gave Himself up for us. Our eternal salvation was more important and the reason for which He came.

"But God demonstrates His own love for us in this: While we were still sinners, Christ died for us." (Romans 5:8).

17

Salvation

"For the wages of sin is death, but the gift of God is eternal life in Christ Jesus our Lord." (Romans 6:23) Without Jesus Christ as your personal Lord and Savior, you are condemned to an eternity in hell.

"For God so loved the world that He gave His One and Only Son, that whoever believes in Him shall not perish but have eternal life. For God did not send His Son into the world to condemn the world but to save the world through Him. Whoever believes in Him is not condemned, but whoever does not believe stands condemned already because He has not believed in the name of God's One and Only Son." (John 3:16-18) But our Almighty Father in heaven does not want anyone to perish.

"For God did not appoint us to suffer wrath but to receive salvation through our Lord Jesus Christ. He died for us so that, whether we are awake or asleep, we may live together with Him." (I Thessalonians 5:9-10)

Calvary is all about love and forgiveness so great that it brings salvation and an eternity in heaven with God our Father to all who believe.

"Everyone who calls on the name of the Lord will be saved." Through the death of Jesus Christ, upon believing in Him and receiving Him, we have eternal life. (Romans 10:13).

"Salvation is found in no one else, for there is no other name under heaven given to men by which we must be saved." (Acts 4:12)

Salvation is found in no one else, only in Jesus. Many people who are not saved have trouble with this. I have heard people ask, "What about all the people who died before Jesus came?" Well, here is your answer. Jesus was always there.

"Then God said, 'Let us make man in our image, in our likeness." (Genesis 1:26) The word says 'our' meaning more than one. The Trinity was always there. "Above the expanse over their heads was what looked like a throne of sapphire, and high above on the throne was a figure like that of a man." (Ezekiel 1:26)

Jesus prayed in (John 17:20-24) "My prayer is not for them alone. I pray also for those who will believe in Me through their message, that all of them may be one, Father, just as you are in Me and I am in you. May they also be in Us so that the world may believe that you have sent Me. I have given them the glory that you gave Me, that they may be one as We are one! I in them and You in Me. May they be brought to complete unity to let the world know that You sent Me and have loved them even as You have loved Me. Father, I want those you have given Me to be with Me where I am and to see My glory, the glory you have given Me because You loved Me before the creation of the world."

He wanted people to believe in Him and that He always existed. "He is the image of the invisible God, the firstborn over all creation. For by Him, all things were created: things in heaven and on earth, visible and invisible, whether thrones or powers or rulers or authorities; all things were created by Him and for Him. He is before all things, and in Him all things hold together." (Colossians 1:15-17)

As long as people believed in God and loved Him and His Word, they also loved Jesus, because He was the Word, who became flesh. These verses tell you that Jesus was always there:

"In the beginning was the Word, and the Word was with God, and the Word was God. He was with God in the beginning." (John 1:1-2)

"The Word became flesh and made His dwelling among us. We have seen His glory, the glory of the One and Only who came from the Father, full of grace and truth." (John 1:14)

The sin of man became so great due to the sinful nature of man, and man trying to follow the law alone. "For when we were controlled by the sinful nature, the sinful passions aroused by the law were at work in our bodies, so that we bore fruit for death." (Romans 7:5)

To save us from our sins so that we would be with Him in eternity He became sin for us. "God made Him who had no sin to be sin for us so that in Him we might become the righteousness of God." (II Corinthians 5:21)

As told in the Book of Leviticus, the blood of a male animal without defect was offered up to the Lord through burnt offerings to make atonement for the sins of the people. When Jesus came He offered Himself, so through the sacrifice of His blood atonement is made once and for all.

"Unlike other the high priests, He does not need to offer sacrifices day after day, first for His own sins, and then for the sins of the people. He sacrificed for their sins once for all when He offered Himself." (Hebrews 7:27)

"My command is this: Love each other as I have loved you. Greater love has no one than this that he lay down his life for his friends." (John 15:12-13)

Through our belief in Him and receiving His forgiveness and Him into our hearts, we are crucified with Him, dying to sin. As He was raised from the dead, so are we.

"If we have been united with Him like this in His death, we will certainly also be united with Him in His resurrection. For we know that our old self was crucified with Him so that the body of sin might be done away with, that we should no longer be slaves to sin--because anyone who has died has been freed from sin." (Romans 6:5-7).

We die to sin and are "born again" to a life with the Spirit of Jesus within us and the fruit of His Spirit, which tells us we are His and keeps us strong and able to endure. For He says, (Joshua 1:5) "I will never leave you nor forsake you." Therefore Jesus truly takes away the sins of the world, before and after He came. He is the only way there is to get to the Father.

(John 1:29) "Look, the Lamb of God, who takes away the sins of the world!"

(John 14:6) "I am the way and the truth and the life. No one comes to the Father except through Me."

The Bible clearly states that Jesus always existed; you only need to read it and you will find out the truths and promises of God.

(Romans 1:20) "For since the creation of the world God's invisible qualities--His eternal power and divine nature--have been clearly seen, being understood from what has been made, so that men are without excuse."

Through believing in and loving God, the people who lived before Jesus came, loved Jesus as well and therefore were saved.

"For all have sinned and fall short of the glory of God and are justified freely by His grace through the redemption that came by Christ Jesus. God presented Him as a sacrifice of atonement, through faith in His blood. He did this to demonstrate His justice because in His forbearance he had left the sins committed beforehand unpunished--He did it to demonstrate His justice at the present time, so as to be just and the One who justifies those who have faith in Jesus." (Romans 3:23-26)

The people who cannot understand that Jesus was, is, and always will be, are of the world and are blinded by Satan.

"The god of this age has blinded the minds of unbelievers so that they cannot see the light of the gospel of the glory of Christ, who is the image of God." (II Corinthians 4:4)

Without Jesus and His Spirit living within them, unbelievers cannot understand the truths of God.

"The man without the Spirit does not accept the things that come from the Spirit of God, for they are foolishness to him, and he cannot understand them, because they are spiritually discerned." (I Corinthians 2:14).

God says that those of us that are His, hear His words and know Him.

"He who belongs to God hears what God says. The reason you do not hear is that you do not belong to God." (John 8:47).

Jesus always existed since the beginning of creation; the Word says so, you just need to look to the Word and you will know that it is true. For great is the Father's love!

(Psalm 36:5) "Your love, O Lord, reaches to the heavens, your faithfulness to the skies."

From the beginning, when sin was brought into the world through Adam and Eve, God knew that we would need a Savior.

(II Thessalonians 2:13-14) "But we ought always to thank God for you, brothers loved by the Lord, because from the beginning God chose you to be saved through the sanctifying work of the Spirit and through belief in the truth. He called you to this through our gospel that you might share in the glory of our Lord Jesus Christ."

God wants all men to be saved; He wants us all with Him in heaven. That was the whole reason for sending Jesus Christ and why we as Christians should pray for and witness to lost souls.

"This is good and pleases God our Savior, who wants all men to be saved and to come to knowledge of the truth." (I Timothy 2:3-4)

Through Jesus, God provided a way of forgiveness for us so that we might have eternal life in heaven.

"Sing to the Lord a new song, for He has done marvelous things; His right hand and His holy arm have worked salvation for Him. The Lord has made His salvation known and revealed His righteousness to the nations." (Psalm 98:1-2)

Through faith in Jesus Christ, we are the righteousness of God. "The righteousness of God comes through faith in Jesus Christ to all who believe." (Romans 3:22).

In the Book of Esther, King Xerxes divorced Queen Vashti and Esther became the new queen of Persia. Haman was plotting to have the Jews killed. Mordecai, Esther's cousin, warned Esther because they were both Jews. Esther had not revealed her nationality to the king, but she had found favor in the king's eyes and she had to chance telling him to save her people. She had to "stand in the gap" to protect her people. This is what Jesus Christ did for us when He died on the cross.

"My soul finds rest in God alone; my salvation comes from Him. He alone is my rock and my salvation; He is my fortress, I will never be shaken." (Psalm 62:1-2).

Just as Haman was trying to kill the Jews, Satan tries to do the same to everyone who had not received Jesus. He keeps telling them lies, along with keeping them in a spiritual prison of heartache and despair. So, along with him, they, too, will suffer eternal damnation. But once you receive Jesus, He protects you and nothing can take you away from Him.

"My sheep listen to My voice; I know them, and they follow Me. I give them eternal life, and they shall never perish; no one can snatch them out of My hand. My Father, who has given them to Me, is greater than all; no one can snatch them out of My Father's hand. I and the Father are One." (John 10:27-30)

I hear many people say, "I am a good person, God won't send me to hell." You may be a good person, but if you have not received Jesus as your personal Lord and Savior, you will not go to heaven and it is your rejection, that sends you to hell, not the Lord. You send yourself there. The many people who think this for some reason or another are refusing to receive Jesus and make a commitment to Him. Therefore they are rebelling against God and rejecting His Son! How would you feel if your son suffered and died willingly for the crimes someone else committed, to protect that person, and that person rejected you and your son? How would that make you feel to know they did not even show appreciation to you or your son for what he did? Then to top it off, the same person comes to you and wants something from you to help them get started on a new life in a new city! You would ask them if they were out of their mind!

Well, how do you think God feels when you reject Jesus by not receiving His free gift of salvation? You want to go your own way and do whatever you please, whether it is a sin or not, and then you still expect Him to give you an eternity of peace and joy in heaven and you reject His Son. You reject the one who suffered accusations and was nailed to the cross. He had blood running down His face from the crown of thorns on his head for you, the whole world, and me. He did it for our sins so that we would receive forgiveness and be set free!

"Therefore, there is now no condemnation for those who are in Christ Jesus because through Christ Jesus the law of the Spirit of life set me free from the law of sin and death." (Romans 8:1-2).

Not only does it set you free from the power of sin, but your heart feels brand new. "I will give them a heart to know Me, that I am the Lord. They will be My people, and I will be their God, for they will return to Me with all their heart." (Jeremiah 24:7).

You have a peace in your heart that cannot be filled in any other way than by Jesus Christ. "I have told you these things, so that in Me you may have peace. In this world you will have trouble. But take heart! I have overcome the world." (John 16:33)

The only way to get to heaven is through Jesus Christ, to be 'born again.' (John 3:3) "I tell you the truth; no one can see the kingdom of God unless he is born again."

"I tell you the truth; no one can enter the kingdom of God unless he is born of water and the Spirit. Flesh gives birth to flesh, but the Spirit gives birth to spirit." (John 3:5-6)

This means, that upon receiving Jesus, you are filled with the Holy Spirit, your heart is changed and you are made alive in Christ, when before you were dead in your transgressions.

"Now if we died with Christ, we believe that we will also live with Him. For we know that since Christ was raised from the dead, He cannot die again; death no longer has mastery over Him. The death He died, He died to sin once and for all; but the life He lives, He lives to God. In the same way, count yourselves dead to sin but alive to God in Christ Jesus." (Romans 6:8-11).

When you receive Jesus, you receive His Spirit into your heart and the fruit of His Spirit, which makes you a new creation in Christ. You will feel His love and peace within and you will be just as loving to others in return. "Therefore, if anyone is in Christ, he is a new creation; the old has gone, the new has come!" (II Corinthians 5:17).

If you have never received Jesus you may ask, "How do I receive Him?" You must believe in Jesus sincerely in your heart and want Him to be your Lord and Savior. Then you must confess it. "That if you confess with your mouth, 'Jesus is Lord,' and believe in your heart that God raised Him from the dead, you will be saved. For it is with your heart that you believe and are justified, and it is with your mouth that you confess and are saved." (Romans 10:9-10).

As we are now a new creation in Christ, we are to be holy as He is holy. "But now He has reconciled you by Christ's physical body through death to present you holy in His sight, without blemish and free from accusation." (Colossians 1:22).

Through the blood of Jesus, our past sins are gone and we start over, alive in Christ. We are washed clean, and purified through Him. In the Book of Numbers, it tells of how the Israelites had to be separate from anyone who was considered "unclean". This was any person who had a skin disease or was unclean because of a dead body. They had to be put outside the camp until they were purified or made clean again. We are to do the same; we are to put off our old self and be separate from the life of sin we once led.

"Do not lie to each other, since you have taken off your old self with its practices and have put on the new self, which is being renewed in knowledge in the image of its Creator." (Colossians 3:9-10)

"Everyone who confesses the name of the Lord must turn away from wickedness." (II Timothy 2:19)

If you do not, you will give Satan a foothold into your life, just like the mistake the Israelites made. After shaking loose of Satan's hold on you when you received Jesus, why would you want to leave any room at all in your life for him to gain a hold of your heart again? The Lord told the Israelites as they crossed over into the Promised Land to destroy all their enemies. In letting some of them stay, it created a stronghold for them to give Satan a foothold and lure them into his traps. This is exactly what happened. As you read all through the Book of Judges you will see how the Canaanites that were allowed to stay continually caused them to drift away from the Lord and into sin. They continually had enemy strongholds to conquer.

Saul fell into Satan's trap as well when pride got the best of him. He let being king go to his head and he repeatedly disobeyed God. This angered God and He decided to look for another king. The rest of Saul's reign as king was in misery and torment. He was tormented by his jealousy of David. He searched and searched for David in order to kill him, but David loved and obeyed the Lord and the Lord protected David. Saul ended his reign by dying in battle along with his sons, fighting against his enemies.

The Lord says to put off our old self, to put away the sinful life we once lived when we receive Jesus as our Lord and Savior. He says this for our own good and He wants us to be holy. So we won't give Satan a foothold into our hearts and lives.

"Be holy, because I am holy." (I Peter 1:16).

"And do not give the devil a foothold." (Ephesians 4:27).

If you fully obey God, you will not end up with the restless wander that Saul and Cain ended up being due to their sin. A life of sin always has you searching for a peace that can only be found in Jesus Christ. The peace and righteousness you find in Jesus is for an eternity; life on earth is but a breath.

"Lift up your eyes to the heavens, look at the earth beneath; the heavens will vanish like smoke, the earth will wear out like a garment and its inhabitants die like flies. But My salvation will last forever, My righteousness will never fail." (Isaiah 51:6).

In the Book of Ruth, there was a woman named Naomi, who was married to Elimelech and they had two sons. There was a famine in the land, so they moved to Moab. One of their sons married Ruth. Ruth was a Moabite, not a Jew, and the Moabites did not worship God as the Jews did. Elimelech and their two sons died, leaving only Naomi, Ruth, and her other daughter-in-law, Orpah.

Naomi told her daughters-in-law that they could go back to their families when their husbands died. But Ruth vowed to stay with Naomi. She loved her and wanted to be with her and worship her God. The Lord was good to her for this and took care of her and her mother-in-law. Anytime we put the Lord first in our lives and hearts, we will be blessed by the Lord for it.

"Blessed is the man who does not walk in the counsel of the wicked or stand in the way of sinners or sit in the seat of mockers. But his delight is in the law of the Lord, and on His law he meditates day and night. He is like a tree planted by streams of water, which yields its fruit in season and whose leaf does not wither. Whatever he does prospers." (Psalm 1:1-3).

As she believed in God through Naomi, Ruth became a child of God, just like you and me. No matter what you did before, when you receive Jesus Christ and the forgiveness He offers, you become a child of God.

"Yet to all who received Him, to those who believed in His name, He gave the right to become children of God--children born not of natural descent, nor of human decision or a husband's will, but born of God." (John 1:12-13).

God did bless Ruth. She married Boaz, who was a relative of Elimelech. Boaz was a kinsman-redeemer; one who is related by blood to those he redeems. He was a blood relative to Elimelech, Naomi's husband. Jesus Christ is our redeemer, who, through His blood, we have forgiveness of sins and a life everlasting. He is our refuge and our deliverer.

"The salvation of the righteous comes from the Lord; He is their stronghold in time of trouble. The Lord helps them and delivers them from the wicked and saves them; because they take refuge in Him." (Psalm 37:39-40).

The Lord also blessed Ruth in that the lineage to the birth of Jesus started with her. Ruth and Boaz had a son, Obed. Obed was the father of Jesse, who was the father of David.

In the Book of I Samuel, the people wanted a king. The Lord chose Saul. Samuel was a prophet whom the people went to for counsel. Saul's father sent Saul out to find a lost donkey; as he went looking for it, he met Samuel. The Lord told Samuel that Saul was the one to be king. This clearly showed that God was in control directing the footsteps of Saul. Just as He directed Saul's path to meet Samuel, He will direct your path as well. He will convict you and place people in your path to be a witness to you.

"All authority in heaven and on earth has been given to Me. Therefore go and make disciples of all nations, baptizing them in the name of the Father and of the Son and of the Holy Spirit, and teaching them to obey everything I have commanded you. And surely I am with you always, to the very end of the age." (Matthew 28:17-20).

The Lord knows those who are His and those who He has predestined to be His. But, it is still up to you to receive Him.

"In Him, we were chosen, having been predestined according to the plan of Him who works out everything in conformity with the purpose of His will, in order that we who were the first to hope in Christ, might be for the praise of His glory." (Ephesians 1:11-12).

The longer you take to make that decision, the longer it will be until you receive salvation, and the blessings of the Lord, which includes His protection and victory over the trials that you go through. You also chance missing it completely, for only God knows the number of days ordained for you.

"Man's days are determined; you have decreed the number of his months and have set limits he cannot exceed." (Job 14:5).

In receiving the gift of salvation from Jesus Christ, I know from experience, the peace and contentment that you feel within your heart. I know that I am never alone, for He is always with me. No matter what troubles I have faced, I have found that when I trusted Jesus to get me through, I came through victoriously! Through Him, you can overcome and conquer anything Satan throws your way.

In the Book of II Samuel, David was King of Israel. Jerusalem was a fortress city. The Jebusites, who were their enemies, inhabited it. They were proud and did not think King David and his army could take the city. King David told the people that anyone who conquers the Jebusites would have to use the "water shaft" to reach those "lame and blind". They did conquer them and Jerusalem became the City of David. The "water shaft" is a symbol of Jesus, who is our "living water", and the only way to salvation.

"Everyone who drinks this water will be thirsty again, but whoever drinks the water I give him will never thirst. Indeed, the water I give him will become in him a spring of water welling up to eternal life." (John 4:13-14).

The "lame and blind" are those who are lost, and Jesus is the only One who can save the lost and conquer the enemy. Just as you are a child of God, and He loves you and wants you with Him in heaven, He knows that you love your family and want them with you in heaven as well. You can trust the Lord to bring them to repentance. He will direct their steps, to a path that leads them to the Godly sorrow that brings repentance.

"I will lead the blind by ways they have not known, along unfamiliar paths I will guide them; I will turn the darkness into light before them and make the rough places smooth. These are the things I will do; I will not forsake them." (Isaiah 42:16).

"Godly sorrow brings repentance that leads to salvation and leaves no regret, but worldly sorrow brings death." (II Corinthians 7:10).

If you pray for the salvation of your loved ones and do not give up no matter what it looks like, they will be saved, for we live by faith and not by sight. Faith pleases God and He wants to save your loved ones.

"Faith is being sure of what we hope for and certain of what we do not see." (Hebrews 11:1).

In the Book of Acts 16, Paul and Silas were traveling to Philippi. They were going outside the city gate to the river to find a place to pray when met a woman who was a dealer in purple cloth from the city of Thyatira. Her name was Lydia and she was a worshiper of God. The Lord opened her heart. He convicted her and opened the eyes of her heart so she would believe Paul's message. She believed and was saved and so were the members of her household. They also came across a slave girl who had a spirit. She predicted the future for money and earned a lot of money for her owners. The girl followed Paul shouting, "These men are servants of the Most High God, who are telling you the way to be saved."

She kept this up for many days and finally, Paul became troubled at it and prayed in the name of Jesus for the spirit to come out of her, and it did. Her owners were angry at this, for now, she would not be able to earn money for them, and so they had Paul and Silas jailed.

At midnight Paul and Silas were praying and singing hymns to God, and God sent a violent earthquake that shook the foundations of the jail and opened the prison doors. This is what happens when you receive Jesus and let Him into your heart. He sets you free! Your heart is free from the bondage of sin and the heaviness of heart that it gives you.

"For I see that you are full of bitterness and captive to sin." (Acts 8:23).

"He has sent Me to bind up the brokenhearted, to proclaim freedom for the captives and release from darkness for the prisoners." (Isaiah 61:1).

Their chains came loose as well, but they did not leave. The jailer came rushing in and fell trembling before them. He knew they were men of God and that this was the work of God. He asked what he had to do to be saved. They told him, (Acts 16:31) "Believe in the Lord Jesus, and you will be saved--you and your household."

The jailer and his household were all saved. After Paul left Athens he went on to Corinth.

"Then Paul left the synagogue and went next door to the house of Titus Justus, a worshiper of God. Crispus, the synagogue ruler, and his entire household believed in the Lord; and many of the Corinthians who heard him believed and were baptized." (Acts 18:7-8).

All these examples of families being saved are promises from God that you can hold on to, to encourage your heart. As Jesus wanted His disciples and us with Him in heaven, He knows we want our families as well. Keep trusting in the Lord and He will fight for you and save your family.

Do not get discouraged. The Israelites had miracle after miracle performed for them, from the parting of the Red Sea to Manna being dropped from heaven to feed them in the desert, yet this did not change their hearts to believe. The hearts of your loved ones must be willing to receive Jesus. Depending on how much of a stronghold Satan may have over them, this may take a while. But God is patient with them.

If you remember the parable of the farmer and the seeds, the seeds that fell among the rocky places that did not have much soil, sprang up quickly. But, they did not have much soil; the ground was shallow due to the rocks. The plants were scorched and withered because they had no root. This is the way it is with your loved ones. For God's message to take root in their heart and bring about the repentance needed for salvation, this sometimes takes a while.

"The Lord is not slow in keeping His promise, as some understand slowness. He is patient with you, not wanting anyone to perish, but everyone to come to repentance." (II Peter 3:9).

Just as the Lord was patient with you and did not give up on you until you received Him, we must also be patient and steadfast in praying for the salvation of our lost loved ones. Trust the Lord to fight for your family.

"If you do not stand firm in your faith, you will not stand at all." (Isaiah 7:9).

In the Book of II Chronicles, it tells of Jehoshaphat, King of Judah. A vast army was coming up against Judah and Jerusalem. King Jehoshaphat declared a fast and prayed to the Lord. The Lord told him, (II Chronicles 20:15) "Do not be afraid or discouraged because of this vast army. For the battle is not yours, but God's." The Lord told them that they would not have to fight: (II Chronicles 20:17) "You will not have to fight this battle. Take up your positions; stand firm and see the deliverance the Lord will give you, O Judah and Jerusalem."

That is exactly what they did and what we have to do as well: stand firm, keep praying, and trust God to deliver our lost loved ones from Satan's clutches. Praise God, for praise pleases God, as it does when someone praises us for something that we have done.

"May the peoples praise you, O God; may all the peoples praise you. Then the land will yield its harvest, and God, our God, will bless us. God will bless us, and all the ends of the earth will fear Him." (Psalm 67:5-7).

The harvest is a symbol of blessings and answered prayers. It took years of praying every day for my husband and he was finally saved. I just got stubborn. No matter what it took, since God did not give up on me, I was not going to give up on my husband, nor was I going to let Satan have him and I am still praying for him today. If you sow in faith and devotion to the Lord, you will reap a harvest of blessings.

The Israelites sang instead of fought. They all gathered together where the Lord told them and sang, "Give thanks to the Lord, for His love endures forever." Can you imagine what this must have looked like to their enemies? This showed that God was in control. They trusted Him and obeyed Him and He gave them the victory over their enemy. He will do the same for you.

God gave Peter a vision showing him that salvation was for everyone who calls on the name of the Lord and believes in Jesus.

"I now realize how true it is that God does not show favoritism but accepts men from every nation who fear Him and do what is right. You know the message God sent to the people of Israel, telling the good news of peace through Jesus Christ, who is Lord of all." (Acts 10:34-36).

God told Peter to go to Cornelius, who was a God-fearing Gentile. Jews at that time were not supposed to associate with Gentiles, which is why God gave Peter the vision. Peter obeyed the Lord and went to tell Cornelius and his relatives and close friends that were with him, the message of Jesus Christ. They believed and received Jesus.

"When the Gentiles heard this, they were glad and honored the word of the Lord; and all who were appointed for eternal life believed." (Acts 13:48)

They all were baptized in the Holy Spirit. This is how the Gentiles were grafted, or adopted into the family of God.

In the Book of Joshua, Joshua was about to take over the strong city of Jericho. He sent two spies out to look the land over beforehand. They came to the house of a prostitute by the name of Rahab. She had heard of the Israelites and of how God was with them and gave them victory over their enemies. She believed. She hid the two spies until they could leave in safety. In return, they told her that they would spare her and her family's lives as long as they were in her house when they came to take the city over. They told her to hang the scarlet cord that she used to help them escape, out of her window and they would know it was her house and spare their lives.

The scarlet cord represents the blood of Jesus, who through receiving Jesus Christ, by His blood we are saved. Just as Rahab and her family were saved because she believed, your family will be saved as well.

If you believe and keep praying eventually your loved ones will be saved. Just do not give up. Satan will do everything in his power to make you give up. But your Heavenly Father is stronger.

"Great is our Lord and mighty in power; His understanding has no limit." (Psalm 147:5).

"You are awesome, O God, in your sanctuary; the God of Israel gives power and strength to His people. Praise be to God!" (Psalm 68:35)

Not only does the Lord's power and might have no limit, but He will give you the strength to endure. That is why He sent Jesus, so we would have the Holy Spirit to guide us and help us. That is why He gave us His Word. We are fighting a spiritual battle.

"The weapons we fight with are not the weapons of the world. On the contrary, they have divine power to demolish strongholds." (II Corinthians 10:4).

The weapons we have are from God.

"Put on the full armor of God so that you can take your stand against the devil's schemes." (Ephesians 6:11).

The armor of the Lord, as described in Ephesians 6:13-18, is:

1. The belt of truth—Be truthful and sincere, and armed with the truth-- which is the Word of God, deep within your mind and heart."

2. The breastplate of righteousness—the righteousness of Jesus, upon receiving Him into your heart is within you.

3. The gospel of peace—knowledge of the Word of God will help you to know His promises and will for you and how much He loves you. A love so great, it gives you eternal life. This will give you peace and help you to overcome evil attacks so you can keep the peace. As well we are to be peaceful, not start fights. We are

to walk in love. For He says, "Blessed are the peacemakers, for they will be called sons of God." (Matthew 5:9)

4. The shield of faith--Trust and Faith in God will always give you victory, peace, and the strength to endure and guard your heart as well.

5. The helmet of Salvation--This is what you need first and foremost, without Jesus, as your Lord and Savior you will be fighting a losing battle. Knowing that you will spend an eternity in heaven where there will be peace and joy forever, with your Almighty Father, gives you great hope and arms you with the courage you need to go through your trials victoriously. Your faith will help you to guard your mind to the obedience of Jesus Christ. Your daily walk, communication with Him, and the Word of God renews your mind.

6. The Sword of the Spirit--which is the Word of God. The Bible has an answer for every situation. The Bible gives you knowledge, wisdom, and instructions on daily life and the promises of God. Reading and knowing the Word of God will help you fight off Satan and guard your mind. He will always try to distort the Word of God through false prophets and the thoughts he gives you. Knowing the Bible will help you keep Satan in his place. It is also the Holy Spirit, "Apart from Me you can do nothing." The Holy Spirit will remind you of the Word you have read and will bring it to your attention right when you need it! "But the Advocate, the Holy Spirit, whom the Father will send in my name, will teach you all things and will remind you of everything I have said to you." (John 14:26)

7. Pray on all occasions--talking to God will keep you close to Him. A close relationship with God will help you to know that He loves you and will always be there for you.

"Come near to God and He will come near to you." (James 4:8).

He wants us prepared, He loves us and wants to give us victory, but we must first receive Him as Lord of our lives and follow Him.

"Blessed are those who wash their robes, that they may have the right to the tree of life and may go through the gates into the city." (Revelation 22:14).

"Be exalted, O God, above the heavens; let your glory be over all the earth." (Psalm 57:5).

18

∿

Grace

Grace is the act of God's unending abounding love for us. (Ephesians 2:4) "But because of His great love for us, God, who is rich in mercy, made us alive with Christ even when we were dead in transgressions--it is by grace you have been saved."

By the grace of God, through Jesus Christ, we have forgiveness for our sins even though we don't deserve it.

"In Him, we have redemption through His blood, the forgiveness of sins, in accordance with the riches of God's grace that He lavished on us with all wisdom and understanding." (Ephesians 1:7-8).

He loved us so much, that He sent Jesus into the world for us, and the salvation that we receive upon accepting Jesus into our hearts is free! It is a gift! We sinned, but Jesus paid the price for us! How then can anyone doubt the love of God?

"Therefore, since we have been justified through faith, we have peace with God through our Lord Jesus Christ, through whom we have gained access by faith into this grace in which we now stand. And we rejoice in the hope of the glory of God." (Romans 5:1-2).

If you had to build a stairway to heaven on your good works you would never make it. (Romans 3:10-11) "There is no one righteous, not even one; there is no one who understands, no one who seeks God."

This is due to the sinful nature that is within us. It goes back to Adam and Eve when they disobeyed God by eating of the Tree of the Knowledge of Good and Evil.

"For if, by the trespass of the one man, death reigned through that one man, how much more will those who receive God's abundant provision of grace and of the gift of righteousness reign in life through the one man, Jesus Christ." (Romans 5:17).

That is where the love, mercy, and grace of God come in. There is nothing on our own that we can do to earn salvation. It is a gift from God. Through the abounding love of God, we have His grace.

"For it is by grace you have been saved, through faith--and this not from yourselves, it is the gift of God--not by works, so that no one can boast." (Ephesians 2:8-9).

By His grace, He gave His One and Only Son to be the atoning sacrifice for our sins. So, through the blood of Jesus, we have forgiveness of our sins. With the love and Spirit of Jesus in our hearts, He gives us strength to overcome our trials and the power of sin.

"Do not be carried away by all kinds of strange teachings. It is good for our hearts to be strengthened by grace, not by ceremonial foods, which are of no value to those who eat them." (Hebrews 13:9).

We go through many trials and hardships as brothers and sisters of our Lord Jesus Christ. But through it all, we have the gift of the Holy Spirit, who comforts us and guides us as we keep our eyes fixed on Jesus. As we endure and persevere in the trials of life, we do get weary, discouraged, and tired; especially if the road that we are on has been a long one. But it is in those times that God's glory shines through; His strength is made perfect in our weakness. (II Corinthians 12:9) "My grace is sufficient for you, for My power is made perfect in weakness."

Not only does He strengthen us, but by His grace, He supplies our needs as well. (John 1:16-17) "From the fullness of His grace, we have all received one blessing after another. For the law was given through Moses; grace and truth came through Jesus Christ."

By God's grace, He let the Israelites suffer discipline over hundreds of years of constant sin and rebellion. He disciplined them instead of leading them back into captivity. They kept on sinning and worshiping other gods, but God's love was greater than their sin. How awesome! After years and years of rebellion, God finally had enough. But He still showed His love and mercy for them because instead of destroying them, He led them back into captivity. How great is the Father's love! (I John 3:1) "How great is the love the Father has lavished on us, that we should be called children of God!"

In seeing how through hundreds of years of sin and rebellion, God kept forgiving the Israelites we see another part of God's grace. By God's grace, we have mercy and compassion when we don't deserve it.

(Hebrews 4:16) "Let us then approach the throne of grace with confidence, so that we may receive mercy and find grace to help us in our time of need."

We also see yet another part of God's grace in this: understanding. By God's grace, we have understanding even when we don't deserve it.

"Do you not know? Have you not heard? The Lord is the everlasting God, the Creator of the ends of the earth. He will not grow tired or weary, and His understanding no one can fathom." (Isaiah 40:28).

By God's grace, we have joy and peace in our hearts where pain and sorrow once dwelt.

"May the God of hope fill you with all joy and peace as you trust in Him, so that you may overflow with hope by the power of the Holy Spirit." (Romans 15:13).

By the love and the grace of God, He will be there for you and lift you up no matter what you are going through. I have lived with so much pain and heartache in my life, that if it were not for the love of God, I would be in a pit of depression. God has picked up the pieces of my broken heart so many times and glued it back together with His love and peace. His love alone keeps me going. The love and understanding that He has shown me through all this, and how He gently corrects me and gets me back on track, has shown how deep His love for us really is. By His grace, He loves us when we are hurting, when we doubt Him, and when we sin against Him.

"And so we know and rely on the love God has for us. God is love.

Whoever lives in love lives in God, and God in him. In this way, love is made complete among us so that we will have confidence on the Day of Judgment because in this world we are like Him. There is no fear in love. But perfect love drives out fear because fear has to do with punishment. The one who fears is not made perfect in love." (I John 4:16-18).

He reminds me of the loved ones that I still have here and that still need me. The love and encouragement that I receive from Him enables me to pass it on not only to my family but to others as well.

"May our Lord Jesus Christ himself and God our Father, who loved us and by His grace gave us eternal encouragement and good hope, encourage your hearts and strengthen you in every good deed and word." (II Thessalonians 2:16).

In receiving God's grace, we learn to be submissive to Him out of our desire to love and please Him. Being submissive to God helps us to develop the gentleness that He wants us all to have for one another, just as He is with us. Just as Jesus came to serve, we as Christians need to serve as well, humbling ourselves. In humbling ourselves to make Jesus the Lord of our lives, and by obeying Him, by His grace we are victorious!

"God opposes the proud but gives grace to the humble." (James 4:6).

"He gives us the victory through our Lord Jesus Christ." (I Corinthians 15:57).

By God's grace, He gives us different gifts to equip us to serve others and to help us in witnessing in any way we can to save lost souls. (Romans 12:6) "We have different gifts, according to the grace given us."

Our gifts, as long as we use them will help us through our trials and give us victory as well. David was loving and compassionate, the people saw this in him and how God loved him and they loved him in return. David loved, trusted, and obeyed God and God gave him victory over all his enemies. (II Samuel 8:6) "The Lord gave David victory wherever he went."

The Lord will give you victory as well, over your enemies, whether it is a spiritual battle in living with a lost loved one or financial or health troubles. Obedience, love, and trust in the Lord will bring you victory in the same way. It will also help you to live the holy life that He wants you to live.

"For the grace of God that brings salvation has appeared to all men. It teaches us to say 'No' to ungodliness and worldly passions, and to live self-controlled, upright, and godly lives in this present age, while we wait for the blessed hope--the glorious appearing of our great God and Savior, Jesus Christ, who gave Himself for us to redeem us from all wickedness and to purify for Himself a people that are His very own, eager to do what is good." (Titus 2:11-14).

He helps you to do this by His love and grace through our Lord Jesus Christ.

"But join with me in suffering for the gospel, by the power of God, who has saved us and called us to a holy life--not because of anything we have done but because of His own purpose and grace. This grace was given us in Christ Jesus before the beginning of time, but it has now been revealed through the appearing of our Savior, Christ Jesus, who has destroyed death and has brought life and immortality to light through the gospel." (II Timothy 1:9-10).

Noah was a righteous man, and blameless among the people of his time in the eyes of the Lord. He walked with God, meaning he loved and obeyed Him. But throughout the earth, man's wickedness increased and this angered God and so He decided to send a flood so great that it would wipe out mankind. But by His grace, He spared Noah's life and that of his family.

I am sure you have all heard the story of Sodom and Gomorrah. The people of Sodom and Gomorrah were wicked and sinned greatly against the Lord. The Lord was angered at this as well and had decided to destroy the two cities. But Abraham's nephew Lot and his family lived in Sodom. Abraham prayed to God on behalf of Lot and his family.

The Lord sent two angels to Lot and his family to tell them to leave the city and not to look back. They told them that the Lord was going to destroy Sodom and Gomorrah due to the extreme wickedness of the people there. By the grace of God, He spared the life of Lot and his family, but as the angels told them not to look back, Lot's wife looked back and turned into a pillar of salt.

As we leave our life of sin and enter into a life of righteousness through our Lord Jesus Christ and the blessings He gives us through His abounding love and compassion, we should never want to go back to our old life of sin. It only leads to destruction. But as Noah and Lot and the rest of their families loved, trusted, and obeyed the Lord, He saved their lives. He saves ours as well through Jesus Christ.

"We believe it is through the grace of our Lord Jesus that we are saved, just as they are." (Acts 15:11).

Abraham was devoted to God. How many of us could show the kind of faith that he showed concerning his only son, Isaac? In testing his faith, God told Abraham to offer up his son, Isaac as a sacrifice to Him. Abraham, being devoted to God, obeyed, trusting in God's love. God spared Isaac as a result of that awesome show of faith. Through his faith, the Lord made a covenant with him blessing all his descendants.

"I will surely bless you and make your descendants as numerous as the stars in the sky and as the sand on the seashore. Your descendants will take possession of the cities of their enemies, and through your off-spring, all nations on earth will be blessed, because you have obeyed me." (Genesis 22:17-18).

Through this covenant and our faith in Jesus Christ, we are heirs of Abraham.

"Therefore, the promise comes by faith, so that it may be by grace and may be guaranteed to all Abraham's offspring--not only to those who are of the law but also to those who are of the faith of Abraham. He is the father of us all. As it is written: 'I have made you a father of many nations.' He is our father in the sight of God, in whom he believed--the God who gives life to the dead and calls things that are not as though they were." (Romans 4:16-17).

The offering up of Isaac was a symbol of what was to come and so was the lamb God provided as an offering in place of Isaac. God provided the lamb as He provided Jesus Christ.

"The Word became flesh and made his dwelling among us. We have seen His glory, the glory of the One and Only, who came from the Father, full of grace and truth." (John 1:14).

The lamb represented Jesus Christ. As the lamb replaced Isaac, Jesus Christ was sacrificed in our place of us. The Lord knew man's heart and sinful nature and had a plan all along.

"For He chose us in Him before the creation of the world to be holy and blameless in His sight. In love, He predestined us to be adopted as His sons through Jesus Christ, in accordance with His pleasure and will-- to the praise of His glorious grace, which He has freely given us in the One He loves." (Ephesians 1:4-6).

We were chosen by His grace, not by our works, to receive His grace and the gift of His salvation.

"So too, at the present time there is a remnant chosen by grace. And if by grace, then it is no longer by works; if it were, grace would no longer be grace." (Romans 11:5-6).

By God's grace, we have eternal life and love everlasting. He pours out His Holy Spirit on us to help us through life; He supplies all our needs, forgives us, and blesses us in some way every day, more than any of us deserve. He gives this all by His wonderful, abounding, never-ending love and grace. All of this is through our Lord and Savior Jesus Christ.

"He saves us through the washing of rebirth and renewal by the Holy Spirit, whom He poured out on us generously through Jesus Christ our Savior, so that, having been justified by His grace, we might become heirs having the hope of eternal life." (Titus 3:5-7).

God's "amazing grace", how sweet it is!

19

~

Sealed & The Holy Spirit

(John 14:15-17) "If you love Me, you will obey what I command. And I will ask the Father, and He will give you another Counselor to be with you forever--the Spirit of truth. The world cannot accept Him, because it neither sees Him nor knows Him, for He lives with you and will be in you." God loved us so much that He wanted to give us all that we would need to enable us to live a holy life here on earth, and then be able to spend eternity with Him in heaven. (John 14:25-26) "All this I have spoken while still with you. But the Counselor, the Holy Spirit, whom the Father will send in My name, will remind you of everything I have said to you."

He not only sent Jesus to be the atonement for our sins but upon His resurrection into heaven, His Holy Spirit was then made possible to be sent into every heart of every person who received Jesus Christ. (II Corinthians 5:21) "God made Him who had no sin to be sin for us so that in Him we might become the righteousness of God." The Holy Spirit reveals and enlightens us to the truths of God. This helps us to understand His Word and His will for our lives. (I Corinthians 2:9-10) "No eye has seen, no ear has heard no mind has conceived what God has prepared for those who love Him but God has revealed it to us by His Spirit."

Upon receiving Jesus Christ into your heart and forgiveness of your sins, you are called to be baptized. (Acts 2:38) "Repent and be baptized, every one of you, in the name of Jesus Christ for the forgiveness of your sins. And you will receive the gift of the Holy Spirit." This is an outward showing that you believe and accept Jesus Christ as your personal Lord and Savior. (I Peter 3:20-22) "In it, only a few people were saved through water, and this water symbolizes baptism that now saves you also--not the removal of dirt from the body but the pledge of a good conscience toward God. It saves you by the resurrection of Jesus Christ, who has gone into heaven and is at God's right hand--with angels, authorities, and powers in submission to Him." We are also called to be baptized by the example that Jesus Himself set for us. (John 13:15-17) "I have set you an example that you should do as I have done for you. I tell you the truth, no servant is greater than his master, nor is a messenger greater than the one who sent him. Now that you know these things, you will be blessed if you do them."

The Lord sent the Holy Spirit to convict the world of sin, and also to convict Christians in their everyday lives when they fall and sin against the Lord. (John 16:7-8) "Unless I go away, the Counselor will not come to you; but if I go, I will send Him to you. When He comes, He will convict the world of guilt in regard to sin and righteousness and judgment." It is Jesus Christ Himself who baptizes you with the Holy Spirit. (John 1:33-34) "The man on whom you see the Spirit come down and remain is He who will baptize with the Holy Spirit. I have seen and I testify that this is the Son of God." Man baptizes you with water, and Jesus baptizes you with the Spirit. (Luke 3:16) "He will baptize you with the Holy Spirit and with fire."

In the Book of I Samuel, Samuel is telling Saul that the Lord has chosen him to be king. In telling Him how the Spirit of the Lord will come upon him and change him is how we are changed upon being baptized in the Holy Spirit. (I Samuel 10:6) "The Spirit of the Lord will come upon you in power, and you will prophesy with them, and you will be changed into a different person." The Holy Spirit of the Lord in us sanctifies us. (II Thessalonians 2:13) "God chose you to be saved through the sanctifying work of the Spirit and through belief in the truth." Being washed in the blood of Jesus, our sins are forgiven and we are now holy in the sight of God. Jesus was holy and was without sin, so in turn, when we receive Him, we are as well. (John 17:17-19) "Sanctify them by the truth; Your Word is truth. As you sent Me into the world, I have sent them into the world. For them, I sanctify Myself, that they too may be truly sanctified."

The Holy Spirit within us helps us to continue to be holy. The Holy Spirit will lead and guide you through all your trials through the still small voice of the Lord within your heart. (John 16:13) "But when He, the Spirit of truth comes, He will guide you into all truth. He will not speak on His own; He will speak only what He hears, and He will tell you what is yet to come."

We have to 'die' to our sinful nature as long as we are in this world every day. Through the trials we go through, as we depend on God and spend time with Him in prayer and through reading His Word, we grow closer to God. We learn the truths and promises that He reveals to us in His Word. That, the spiritual gifts given to us by the Lord, and the fruit of His Spirit help us to endure and persevere through our trials, and to help others in their trials. (Romans 5:2-5) "And we rejoice in the hope of the glory of God. Not only so, but we also rejoice in our sufferings, because we know that suffering produces perseverance; perseverance, character; character, and hope. And hope does not disappoint us, because God has poured out His love into our hearts by the Holy Spirit, whom He has given us."

Our Heavenly Father sends the Holy Spirit, and the fruit of the Spirit indwells in us, upon receiving Jesus into our hearts. (Galatians 5:22-23) "But the fruit of the Spirit is love, joy, peace, patience, kindness, goodness, faithfulness, gentleness and self-control." This is how in Christ we are a new creation, the fruit of His Spirit within us, and going through our trials, we are changed into who God wants us to be. (Hebrews 10:10) "And by that will, we have been made holy through the sacrifice of the body of Jesus Christ once and for all."

In the Book of II Kings, the men of the city of Jericho told Elisha that the water was bad and the land was unproductive. This is how we all are before we receive Jesus. We are not filled with the fruit of His Spirit and therefore we bear no fruit. Our life is not a light to the world. Elisha told them to bring him a 'new bowl' in which he put salt in it and threw it into the spring. The water was healed. In receiving Jesus, that 'new bowl' is us as a new creation in Christ. We are called to be the 'salt of the earth.' (Mark 9:49-50) "Everyone will be salted with fire. Salt is good, but if it loses its saltiness, how can you make it salty again? Have salt in yourselves, and be at peace with each other." Our lives are supposed to show people in the way we live that we are Spirit-filled Christians by the fruit of the Spirit of Jesus within us. Therefore our life should be a witness to the world that Jesus does exist and that Jesus is the Lord of our lives. The Holy Spirit gives life to your soul and we are called to witness and testify to that life.

As the Lord told Moses in the Book of Deuteronomy, to choose a place for Him to dwell, through Jesus He dwells within your heart. And as He traveled with the Israelites in a cloud by day and a pillar of fire at night, so will the Holy Spirit be with you. The Holy Spirit will lead you, guide you, and comfort you as well. (II Corinthians 1:3-4) "Praise be to the God and Father of our Lord Jesus Christ, the Father of compassion and the God of all comfort, who comforts us in all our troubles so that we can comfort those in any trouble with the comfort we ourselves have received from God."

Learning the promises of God, how much He loves you, and through the gifts and guidance of the Holy Spirit helps us to be the witnesses that we are all called to be. (Mark 16:15-18) "Go into all the world and preach the good news to all creation. Whoever believes and is baptized will be saved, but whoever does not believe will be condemned. And these signs will accompany those who believe: In My name, they will drive out demons; they will speak in tongues; they will pick up snakes with their hands; and when they drink deadly poison, it will not hurt them at all; they will place their hands on sick people, and they will get well."

In the Book of Acts, it tells of how Paul was converted and began to preach the word of God boldly! This is from someone who used to persecute Christians! Now he was trying to lead people to salvation to become Christians! (Acts 4:31) "After they prayed, the place where they were meeting was shaken. And they were all filled with the Holy Spirit and spoke the Word of God boldly." This is how the Holy Spirit also strengthens you and changes you. (Ephesians 3:16-17) "I pray that out of His glorious riches, He may strengthen you with power through His Spirit in your inner being, so that Christ may dwell in your hearts through faith." The Holy Spirit within us strengthens us and encourages us. You can feel the presence of His Spirit within you, and knowing that He is there, that He loves you, and will guide you helps to increase your faith, bringing peace to your heart. (Acts 9:31) "Then the Church throughout Judea, Galilee, and Samaria enjoyed a time of peace. It was strengthened; and encouraged by the Holy Spirit; it grew in numbers, living in the fear of the Lord."

When we ask Jesus into our hearts we are indwelt with His Spirit, and at His appointed time He will baptize us with His Holy Spirit or we receive the power of the Holy Spirit. (Acts 11:16) "John baptized with water, but you will be baptized with the Holy Spirit." Just as God anointed Saul, David, and Paul with the power of the Holy Spirit, you can be too. (Luke 11:13) "If you then, though you are evil, know how to give good gifts to your children, how much more will your Father in heaven give the Holy Spirit to those who ask Him?" God wants everyone to be a witness for Him, and we are not to be ashamed of it. (Mark 8:38) "If anyone is ashamed of Me and My Words in this adulterous and sinful generation, the Son of Man will be ashamed of him when He comes in His Father's glory with the holy angels."

In being baptized with the Holy Spirit, as I quoted earlier in Mark 16:15-18 and Luke 3:16, there will be signs that accompany the baptism. (I Corinthians 14:22) "Tongues, then, are a sign, not for believers but for unbelievers; prophecy, however, is for believers, not for unbelievers." (Acts 2:4) "All of them were filled with the Holy Spirit and began to speak in other tongues as the Spirit enabled them."

Many people think that these things do not happen today, that it was just in the days of Paul and the rest of the Apostles, that is not so. Some use this verse as a reference, (I Corinthians 13:8-10) "Love never fails. But where there are prophecies, they will cease; where there are tongues, they will be stilled; where there is knowledge, it will pass away. For we know in part and we prophesy in part, but when perfection comes, the imperfect disappears." Jesus was perfect. But Paul is speaking here after Jesus had already come! He is talking about our own perfection. For here on earth as we live in the human body, we will always 'fall short.'

We will not reach perfection until we get to heaven. Neither was he speaking of the completion of the New Testament. Paul was writing as the Spirit led him to instruct the people of the different places he traveled to. He did not even know that he was writing the New Testament.

We need to take all Scripture together, not just in parts. (Philippians 3:10-14) "I want to know Christ and the power of His resurrection and the fellowship of sharing in His sufferings, becoming like Him in His death, and so, somehow, to attain the resurrection from the dead. Not that I have already obtained all this, or have already been made perfect, but I press on to take hold of that for which Christ Jesus took hold of me. Brothers, I do not consider myself yet to have taken hold of it. But one thing I do: Forgetting what is behind and straining toward what is ahead, I press on toward the goal to win the prize for which God has called me heavenward in Christ Jesus."

We will not reach perfection until we get to heaven, until then we need all the spiritual gifts that the Lord wants to bless us with. We need them to help increase our knowledge and wisdom of the Bible, to help us with our Christian walk on earth, and to help us in witnessing to others, leading them to the wonderful gift of salvation! Just as the Spirit of Jesus never changes, neither does His Spirit within us or the gifts that He gives us. (Hebrews 13:8) "Jesus Christ is the same yesterday and to-day and forever." If Jesus is the same yesterday, today, and forever, so is His Holy Spirit and the anointing He places on everyone born into the family of God.

If you read in the Book of Leviticus, it talks about Pentecost. Pentecost is celebrated 50 days after the night of Passover. The Passover was celebrated when the Israelites were in bondage to the Egyptians.

Everyone who had the blood of a year-old lamb without defect smeared over the top and sides of their door frames would be safe. The angel of the Lord was to pass through the streets, and every firstborn child of any family that did not have this on their doors would be put to death. All the Israelites were warned of this, and if they obeyed their lives would be spared, just as you and me are warned of the consequences of living a life of sin. It is an eternity in hell. God loves us and warns us of this, and tells us what to do to be saved. If we do not heed His warnings, it is our fault and not His.

Passover represents leaving our life of sin behind, dying to our sins, and being born again into the family of God. Just as the Lord saved them from death, He saves us from eternal damnation. He did that when He died on the cross at Calvary. Pentecost represents the deliverance of the people from their bondage of slavery to the Egyptians, just as every one of us who receives Jesus is delivered from the bondage of sin. We are harvested into the family of God. During the celebration of Pentecost, they were to offer a burnt offering and a drink offering. This burnt offering represents the body and blood of Jesus Christ who was offered up for our sins. They were also to offer a first fruit offering, which also represents Jesus who was our first fruit. He was the first to rise from the dead and upon His resurrection into heaven, His Holy Spirit was made available to all who believe and receive.

We receive the fruit of His Spirit, and first, also represents our devotion to Him, we are to put Him first. Greet the day and end the day talking to the Lord, just as the Israelites were to offer up a sin offering in the morning and in the evening. We are also to give Him the first fruits of our pay. Not second. He is the One who provides us with work and supplies all our needs. We are to trust Him for that. (Psalm 23:1-2) "The Lord is my Shepherd; I shall not be in want. He makes me lie down in green pastures, He leads me beside quiet waters, He restores my soul." If you are not in want, then there is nothing that you need. All your needs are met.

Many people are confused about the baptism of the Holy Spirit and wonder what happens to you at conversion. (Matthew 28:19-20)

"Therefore go and make disciples of all nations, baptizing them in the name of the Father and of the Son and of the Holy Spirit, and teaching them to obey everything I have commanded you. And surely I am with you always, to the very end of the age." (II Corinthians 13:14) "May the grace of the Lord Jesus Christ, and the love of God, and the fellowship of the Holy Spirit be with you all."

At conversion, we are indwelt with the Spirit of Jesus. (Galatians 4:6-7) "Because you are sons, God sent the Spirit of His Son into our hearts, the Spirit who calls out, "*Abba*, Father.' So you are no longer a slave, but a son; and since you are a son, God has made you also an heir." This is a part of being "born again." (John 3:3) "I tell you the truth; no one can see the kingdom of God unless he is born again." We are made alive with Christ in this. (Ephesians 2:4-5) "But because of His great love for us, God, who is rich in mercy, made us alive with Christ even when we were dead in transgressions--it is by grace you have been saved."

Being filled with the Holy Spirit is like drinking a glass of water. The water is in you as you drink it. So it is when you become a Christian and are indwelt with the Spirit of Jesus at conversion. When you are baptized with the Holy Spirit, receiving power from above, it is like being totally immersed in water, like going swimming. When you are underwater you are immersed in it. Another way to look at it is the wiring in the walls of your house. The wiring runs through walls, but if you do not flip the switch on there will not be any light. The Holy Spirit within us at conversion is the wiring and Jesus flipping the switch on is the baptism of the Holy Spirit. Jesus turns on the power to what is already in you. That is what it is to be baptized in the Holy Spirit. We receive His Spirit at conversion, but when we are baptized it is like receiving the second portion of the Spirit.

The Holy Spirit empowers us to speak in tongues, heal people, and drive out demons as the Lord God decides to distribute these gifts to us. (Acts 1:8) "But you will receive power when the Holy Spirit comes on you." When we are obedient to God, submit to His will, and read the Bible, our minds are renewed day by day. (Romans 12:2) "Do not conform any longer to the pattern of this world, but be transformed by the renewing of your mind."

The indwelling of the Spirit of Jesus helps us to walk in the Spirit. The fruit of His Spirit shows through. (Romans 8:9) "You, however, are controlled not by the sinful nature but by the Spirit, if the Spirit of God lives in you. And if anyone does not have the Spirit of Christ, he does not belong to Christ." There is only one baptism of the Holy Spirit. (Ephesians 4:3-6) "Make every effort to keep the unity of the Spirit through the bond of peace. There is one body and one Spirit--just as you were called to one hope when you were called--one Lord, one faith, one baptism; one God and Father of all, who is over all and through all and in all."

When you are born again, God united Himself with you through the Holy Spirit and you become one, thus "one with Him in spirit." (I Corinthians 6:17) "But he who unites himself with the Lord is one with Him in spirit." You are not two beings, but one. (I Corinthians 12:13) "For we were baptized by one Spirit into one body—whether Jews or Greeks slave or free—and we were all given the one Spirit to drink." Being baptized in the Holy Spirit is simply filling you to the fullest and completing what He began. (Colossians 2:9-12) "For in Christ all the fullness of the Deity lives in bodily form, and you have been given fullness in Christ, who is the head over every power and authority. In Him you were also circumcised, in the putting off of the sinful nature not with a circumcision done by the hands of men but with the circumcision done by Christ, having been buried with Him in baptism and raised with Him through your faith in the power of God, who raised Him from the dead."

Jesus Christ does this baptism, not the water baptism done by your Pastor. Baptism of the Holy Spirit is given to us by Jesus Christ, and when He chooses to bestow it on us. It is to turn the power of the Holy Spirit that is already in us. Another explanation is when you put fuel in a car it is in the tank, but the car will not turn on until you turn the key in the ignition switch. Again, Jesus is just flipping the switch. (Matthew 3:11) "I baptize you with water for repentance. But after me will come

One who is more powerful than I, whose sandals I am not fit to carry. He will baptize you with the Holy Spirit and with fire."

As we are obedient and earnestly seek the baptism upon His will, His timing, not ours, we are baptized with the Holy Spirit. (Acts 5:32) "We are witnesses of these things, and so is the Holy Spirit, whom God has given to those who obey Him." As a result of being baptized in the Holy Spirit, you are filled with the Holy Spirit and the His power. (Acts 4:8-10) "Then Peter, filled with the Holy Spirit, said to them: 'Rulers and elders of the people! If we are being called to account today for an act of kindness shown to a cripple and are asked how he was healed, then know this, you and all the people of Israel: it is by the name of Jesus Christ of Nazareth, whom you crucified but whom God raised from the dead, that this man stands before you healed."

In the Old Testament when the Israelites were building the Tabernacle, God did not fill the Tabernacle with His Spirit until the work was completed. (Exodus 40:33-34) "Then Moses set up the courtyard around the tabernacle and altar and put up the curtain at the entrance to the courtyard. And so Moses finished the work. Then the cloud covered the Tent of Meeting, and the glory of the Lord filled the tabernacle." Everything had to be in order. God is not a God of disorder. (I Corinthians 14:33) "For God is not a God of disorder but of peace." That is why in giving Moses the measurements in building the Tabernacle, everything had to be exact. So, it is with us and our walk with God. He will not inhabit anything or anyone unclean. (I Corinthians 6:19-20) "Do you not know that your body is a temple of the Holy Spirit, who is in you, whom you have received from God? You are not your own; you were bought at a price. Therefore honor God with your body."

As you read in the Old Testament you will see that any time anyone died or was diseased, they had to be put outside the city. They were considered "unclean." As our hearts and minds are renewed, at the appropriate time set forth by God, if you do not quit and you keep asking, you will be baptized with the Holy Spirit. Keep obeying God, walking in the fruit of His Spirit, and keep asking Him. You will be baptized because it is a promise for all Christians. (James 4:2) "You do not have, because you do not ask God."

The Israelites were also called to offer a new grain offering at Pentecost as well, a wave offering. As the Jewish people offered up a new grain offering to the Lord, He in turn is our bread of life. (John 6:35) "I am the bread of life. He who comes to Me will never go hungry, and he who believes in Me will never be thirsty." He will not only meet our physical needs, but our spiritual needs as well.

A wave offering signifies fellowship between you and Jesus Christ and the peace you receive once you are saved. The new grain offering consisted of two loaves of bread, made with two-tenths of an ephah of fine flour baked with yeast. These two loaves represent the Jewish people in which Jesus offered salvation to them first and then the Gentiles. They were made with yeast, which represents sin, meaning we can come to Jesus as sinners, ask for forgiveness, and receive His Holy Spirit into our hearts. (Romans 5:8) "But God demonstrates His own love for us in this: While we were still sinners, Christ died for us." They were made with two-tenths of an ephah of fine flour. "Fine flour" is a representation of the perfect, sinless life of Jesus Christ.

It was to be mixed with oil, which is a representation of the Holy Spirit. They were to add salt to their offering as well. (Leviticus 2:13) "Season all your grain offerings with salt. Do not leave the salt of the covenant of your God out of your grain offerings; add salt to all your offerings." Salt is a symbol of the permanence of the Holy Spirit. (Numbers 18:19) "Whatever is set aside from the holy offerings the Israelites present to the Lord I give to you and your sons and daughters as your regular share. It is an everlasting covenant of salt before the Lord for both you and your offspring."

It is also a symbol of the power of the Holy Spirit and how it enlightens you and enables you to speak boldly. (Colossians 4:6) "Let your conversation be always full of grace, seasoned with salt, so that you may know how to answer everyone." (Acts 4:29-30) "Now, Lord, consider their threats and enable your servants to speak your word with great boldness. Stretch out your hand to heal and perform miraculous signs and wonders through the name of your holy servant Jesus." They were also to use two-tenths of an ephah of fine flour. Regular grain offerings were made with only one-tenth. (Leviticus 6:20-21) "A tenth of an ephah of fine flour as a regular grain offering, half of it in the morning and half in the evening. Prepare it with oil on a griddle."

These two-tenths mean a double portion of His Holy Spirit is available to us. Just as Elisha asked Elijah for a double portion of his spirit before Elijah was taken up to heaven. The way Elijah was taken up in a chariot of fire and a whirlwind is the way the Holy Spirit comes on us when we are baptized in the Holy Spirit. Fire and wind symbolize the Holy Spirit. (Acts 2:2-4) "Suddenly a sound like the blowing of a violent wind came from heaven and filled the whole house where they were sitting. They saw what seemed to be tongues of fire that separated and came to rest on each of them. All of them were filled with the Holy Spirit and began to speak in other tongues as the Spirit enabled them." (II Kings 2:9-11) "Let me inherit a double portion of your spirit,' Elisha replied. 'You have asked a difficult thing,' Elijah said, 'yet if you see me when I am taken from you, it will be yours-- otherwise not.' As they were walking along and talking together, suddenly a chariot of fire and horses of fire appeared and separated the two of them, and Elijah went up to heaven in a whirlwind."

We can receive a double portion as well. First at receiving the indwelling of His Spirit into our hearts at conversion, then at the baptism of the Holy Spirit in which we are filled with His Spirit and the power of the Spirit. We just need to see with our hearts and believe. This is what is symbolized when Elijah told Elisha if he saw him when he was taken.

The first baptisms were given to the disciples and then to the people they started preaching to. The disciples had to wait until Jesus ascended into heaven. (Acts 1:4-5) "Do not leave Jerusalem, but wait for the gift My Father promised, which you have heard Me speak about. For John baptized with water, but in a few days you will be baptized with the Holy Spirit." This also shows that Jesus told them to wait. It is up to Jesus when we receive it. Some of the people they preached to, upon believing received the baptism at once. (Acts 2:1-3) "When the day of Pentecost came, they were all together in one place. Suddenly a sound like the blowing of a violent wind came from heaven and filled the whole house where they were sitting. They saw what seemed to be tongues of fire that separated and came to rest on each of them."

This was the beginning of Christianity and people needed to be aware of Jesus and what He offered. The Lord will baptize us according to how He chooses to, big and bold or like a bolt of love and joy hitting our hearts all at once. (Matthew 11:29) "I am gentle and humble in heart, and you will find rest for your souls." As with our faith, some of us are stronger in faith than others. The Lord may use more vivid ways of showing someone with new or weak faith that He is there for them than with someone with strong faith. (Psalm 139:1-4) "O Lord, you have searched me and you know me. You know when I sit and when I rise; you perceive my thoughts from afar. You discern my going out and my lying down; you are familiar with all my ways. Before a word is on my tongue you know it completely, O Lord."

I believe their hunger and willingness to believe, is the reason why the Holy Spirit came on so many people all at once back then and in the way it did. Others did not receive it at the time of their conversion. (Acts 19:1-2) "There he found some disciples and asked them, 'Did you receive the Holy Spirit when you believed?' They answered, 'No, we have not even heard that there is a Holy Spirit." At that, Paul placed his hands on them. (Acts 19:6) "When Paul placed his hands on them, the Holy Spirit came on them, and they spoke in tongues and prophesied."

The baptism of the Holy Spirit is for all who believe. (Acts 3:38-39) "Repent and be baptized, every one of you, in the name of Jesus Christ for the forgiveness of your sins. And you will receive the gift of the Holy Spirit. The promise is for you and your children and for all who are far off--for all whom the Lord our God will call." (Acts 8:14-16) "When the apostles in Jerusalem heard that Samaria had accepted the Word of God, they sent Peter and John to them. When they arrived, they prayed for them that they might receive the Holy Spirit because the Holy Spirit had not yet come upon any of them; they had simply been baptized into the name of the Lord Jesus."

There are reasons why some people have never received the baptism of the Holy Spirit; one is lack of faith. (James 1:6-7) "But when he asks, he must believe and not doubt, because he who doubts is like a wave of the sea, blown and tossed by the wind. That man should not think he will receive anything from the Lord; he is a double-minded man, unstable in all he does." (Hebrews 11:6) "And without faith it is impossible to please God." You must believe in God and the promises He gives us in the Bible. We cannot take bits and pieces of the Bible to believe for our own choosing just because we have never seen some of the things mentioned in the Bible. We have never seen God, yet we believe in Him. What is the difference? That is not what faith is; faith believes without seeing. (Hebrews 10:35-36) "So do not throw away your confidence; it will be richly rewarded. You need to persevere so that when you have done the will of God, you will receive what He has promised." (Hebrews 11:1) "Now faith is being sure of what we hope for and certain of what we do not see."

Another reason may be that Jesus simply does not think you are ready to receive it yet. (Hebrews 5:13-14) "Anyone who lives on milk, being still an infant, is not acquainted with the teaching about righteousness. But solid food is for the mature, who by constant use have trained themselves to distinguish good from evil." (Hebrews 6:1-3) "Therefore let us leave the elementary teachings about Christ and go on to maturity, not laying again the foundation of repentance from acts that lead to death, and of faith in God, instruction about baptisms, the laying on of hands, the resurrection of the dead, and eternal judgment. And God permitting, we will do so."

There are different kinds of gifts all of which are given to us by the grace of God through the Holy Spirit. Some are given to us at the time we receive the Spirit of Jesus within us. Some are not given until we are baptized with the Holy Spirit. This again depends on Jesus, His purpose for you, and if He thinks you are ready for it. How is your love walk, how do you treat people? Is it full of the flesh and the 'what about me's? Love is what compelled Jesus in everything He did and is needed to use the gift of encouragement, service, teaching, hospitality, and the gift of healing. There can be no flesh, Jesus and His purpose and glory is always first. Would you want your 9-year-old child driving your car? No! He is not mature enough, old enough, or experienced enough to handle it. So it is with the gift of the Holy Spirit. If you are not mature enough in your Christian walk, meaning you still have a lot of flesh, you would be more apt to misuse certain powerful gifts, thus not using it for God's glory.

Being baptized in the Holy Spirit is a matter of yielding and faith, not age. Nor is it about how perfect a Christian you are in your daily walk. As long as we live in the flesh, there will be times that we mess up. You will be baptized; it is a promise and a gift, and will come when you persevere in asking, believe God, and you let no fear rule over you. (James 1:2-4) "Consider it pure joy, my brothers, whenever you face trials of many kinds because you know that the testing of your faith develops perseverance. Perseverance must finish its work so that you may be mature and complete, not lacking anything." To be mature in your faith you have been purified, or have undergone the baptism of fire.

"I baptize you with water for repentance. But after me will come one who is more powerful than I, whose sandals I am not fit to carry. He will baptize you with the Holy Spirit and with fire." (Matthew 3:11).

God likens the process of purification to the purifying process of gold. When gold is purified it goes through the fire until the goldsmith can see his image in it. (I Peter 1:3-7) "Praise be to the God and Father of our Lord Jesus Christ! In his great mercy, he has given us new birth into a living hope through the resurrection of Jesus Christ from the dead, and into an inheritance that can never perish, spoil, or fade—kept in heaven for you, who through faith are shielded by God's power until the coming of the salvation that is ready to be revealed in the last time. In this, you greatly rejoice, though now for a little while you may have had to suffer grief in all kinds of trials. These have come so that your faith—of greater worth than gold, which perishes even though refined by fire—may be proved genuine and may result in praise, glory, and honor when Jesus Christ is revealed."

God wants to see His image in you! We should be a reflection of our Lord and Savior! This gives true glory to God; the world is affected more by your life than your words. (II Corinthians 3:18) "And we, who with unveiled faces all reflect the Lord's glory, are being transformed into His likeness with ever-increasing glory, which comes from the Lord, who is the Spirit."

In the Book of Daniel 3:20-27, Shadrach, Meshach, and Abednego are thrown into a fiery furnace and they came forth unharmed! In fact, people saw a fourth man in the fire with them, a man that looks like "a son of the gods." This was Jesus! This passage represents the purification process of God. The Lord has years of the world to "weed" out of most of us when we are saved. (Matthew 15:13) "He replied, "Every plant that my heavenly Father has not planted will be pulled up by the roots." Yes, we are a new creation, but our minds need to be renewed. (Romans 12:2) "Do not conform any longer to the pattern of this world, but be transformed by the renewing of your mind. Then you will be able to test and approve what God's will is—His good, pleasing, and perfect will."

In submitting to the "baptism of fire," God will purify your heart removing the impurities and you will "come forth as gold," and ready to move on to the next stage in your walk giving all glory to God as He deserves. If you want to be greatly used by God as He promises, "You will do even greater things than these" then you will have to go through the fire; if you want to share in the glory in the inheritance, then you have to share in the trials. (Romans 8:17) "Now if we are children, then we are heirs—heirs of God and co-heirs with Christ, if indeed we share in His sufferings in order that we may also share in His glory."

In letting God purify you—you are also learning how to be led by the Spirit. (Galatians 5:24-25) "Those who belong to Christ Jesus have crucified the sinful nature with its passions and desires. Since we live by the Spirit, let us keep in step with the Spirit." This is day-to-day dying to self, meaning not giving in to selfish desires when it goes against God's will. (Luke 9:23) "If anyone would come after Me, he must deny himself and take up his cross daily and follow Me." (Philippians 1:21) "For to me, to live is Christ and to die is gain." If you ever want to be used mightily in your daily life for God, you need to remember it is for His glory and not your own, and you must let the Holy Spirit lead you; not your mind, will, and emotions. This is submitting to the Lordship of Christ. Your flesh and your mind may want to do something contrary to the Spirit, but it is your choice to obey it or God. (I Corinthians 2:15) "The spiritual man makes judgments about all things, but he himself is not subject to any man's judgment: 'For who has known the mind of the Lord that he may instruct Him?' But we have the mind of Christ." You are doing God's will and it is for His purpose and glory. He already knows the outcome, therefore He already knows the process and steps He wants to take to achieve it. The purification process is also known as sanctification. (I Thessalonians 5:23) "May God Himself, the God of peace, sanctify you through and through. May your whole spirit, soul, and body be kept blameless at the coming of our Lord Jesus Christ."

Ignorance of the baptism, fear, and your daily Christian walk lacks love, are three of the biggest hindrances to receiving the baptism of the Holy Spirit. and fear and unbelief go hand in hand. Love is the driving force behind everything God has done for us, and without love, the Holy Spirit will not manifest Himself through you. Having no love blocks the flow of His love working through you. If you are fearful then you are not trusting in God. (Hebrews 11:6) "And without faith it is impossible to please God because anyone who comes to Him must believe that He exists and that He rewards those who earnestly seek Him." Some people may be baptized the moment they are saved while others may be saved for five or ten years before receiving it! Baptism of the Holy Spirit can come to a young child or an adult. John the Baptist was baptized at birth. (Luke 1:11-15) "Then an angel of the Lord appeared to him, standing at the right side of the altar of incense. When Zechariah saw him, he was startled and was gripped with fear. But the angel said to him, 'Do not be afraid, Zechariah; your prayer has been heard. Your wife Elizabeth will bear you a son, and you are to give him the name John. He will be a joy and delight to you, and many will rejoice because of his birth, for he will be great in the sight of the Lord. He is never to take wine or other fermented drink, and he will be filled with the Holy Spirit even from birth."

Acts 2:17 tells of how the Lord will pour out His Spirit on our sons and daughters, and in Matthew 18:3 tells of how we must have the faith of a child because children trust their parents completely. Samuel was just a boy when while at Eli's house learning under his authority, he first heard the voice of the Lord. David was just a young boy when he was anointed to be king and still a young boy when through the help of the Lord defeated Goliath, a man nine feet tall! Age does not matter! It is the willingness to yield and surrender completely to the Holy Spirit and let Him move or speak through you that makes the difference. (Isaiah 42:8) "I am the Lord; that is My name! I will not give My glory to another or My praise to idols." (Romans 12:6) "We have different gifts, according to the grace given us." No matter what gifts that we are blessed with, God works in all of them. (I Corinthians 12:6) "There are different kinds of working, but the same God works all of them in all men." The gifts given to you upon being baptized by the Holy Spirit are for the good of all people, whether it is believers or unbelievers. (I Corinthians 12:7) "Now to each one the manifestation of the Spirit is given for the common good." We are to love one another, and not only in words but in our actions as well. Sometimes the love that you show someone is the only way that they will see Jesus. (Luke 6:31-32) "Do to others as you would have them do to you. If you love those who love you, what credit is that to you?" (I Corinthians 13:13) "And now these three remain: faith, hope, and love. But the greatest of these is love." Not everyone will have the same gift.

"I will pour out My Spirit on all people. Your sons and daughters will prophesy, your old men will dream dreams, and your young men will see visions. Even on My servants, both men and women, I will pour out My Spirit in those days." (Joel 2:28-29).

The gifts of the Spirit are broken down into three Basic Groups, which are: Domata Gifts (equipping the Church or ministries), Charismata Gifts (stewardship gifts or ability gifts), and Pneumatic Charismata Gifts (spiritual gifts for dynamic manifestations of the Holy Spirit in which He openly displays Himself). There are three categories within the Pneumatic Charismata Gifts found in I Corinthians 12, which are the major gifts: Revelation Gifts, Vocal Gifts, and Power Gifts. You need complete faith to operate in these gifts. The Revelation Gifts are: Word of

Wisdom, Word of Knowledge, and Discerning of spirits; the Vocal Gifts are: speaking in tongues, interpretation of tongues, and gifts of prophecy (dreams and visions fall into this category and are found in Acts 2:17-18). If someone who speaks in tongues in Church an interpreter must be present. It is to edify or build up the church. (I Corinthians 14:5) "I would like every one of you to speak in tongues, but I would rather have you prophesy. He who prophesies is greater than the one who speaks in tongues, unless he interprets, so that the church may be edified." If one speaks in tongues in private to himself as in praying to or praising God, it builds up his faith. (I Corinthians 14:4) "He who speaks in a tongue edifies himself, but he who prophesies edifies the church." This only gives you a greater awareness that you are filled with the Holy Spirit, which increases your faith in knowing that God is with you and loves you. The Power Gifts are faith, healing, and miracles. It does not matter what gift you have, each one is needed and important. In Christ, we are all the 'body of Christ' and each part is needed to make it all complete. (I Corinthians 12:12-13) "The body is a unit, though it is made up of many parts; and though all its parts are many, they form one body. So it is with Christ. For we were all baptized by one Spirit into one body--whether Jews or Greeks, slave or free--and we were all given the one Spirit to drink."

God gives us the spiritual gifts that best fit us, and we are all to work together for the good of all people and for the unity of the whole body of Christ. (I Corinthians 12:24-26) "But God has combined the members of the body and has given greater honor to the parts that lacked it, so that there should be no division in the body, but that its parts should have equal concern for each other. If one part suffers, every part suffers with it; if one part is honored, every part rejoices with it."

In using any of our gifts it is not for our own good. It is to bring glory to God, to witness to unbelievers, and to strengthen the church. As the church is strengthened, it is able to do more of a service to all people in the way God intended it to be. (I Corinthians 14:26) "What then shall we say, brothers? When you come together, everyone has a hymn, or a word of instruction, a revelation, a tongue, or an interpretation. All of these must be done for the strengthening of the church."

The different spiritual gifts or callings given by the Lord are found in the Book of Acts, Romans, I Corinthians, and Ephesians. In the Book of Romans 12, and I Corinthian 12, lists the Charismata Gifts, or steward-ship gifts, such as teaching, serving, giving (being generous), encourage-ment, and leadership. It also tells of how we are all to be hospitable. It lists the gifts of administration and the gift of helping others. The gifts listed in the Book of Ephesians are the Domata Gifts, or Gifts of Office, which are evangelists, pastors, and apostles.

Out of God's overwhelming love for us as He calls each of us into the ministry He has for us and He anoints us to perform it. (I John 2:20) "But you have an anointing from the Holy One, and all of you know the truth." We are given an anointing for the call on our life that He has for us. This anointing is the ability to do whatever task or ministry that He has for us. (I John 2:27) "As for you, the anointing you received from Him remains in you, and you do not need anyone to teach you. But as His anointing teaches you about all things and as that anointing is real, not counterfeit--just as it has taught you, remain in Him."

The ability will be easy for us, but for someone else, it may be difficult, just like David when he was about to go up against Goliath. King Saul gave him his armor and it did not fit. The anointing God has for me will not be like the anointing He has for you. The calling He has for you may be to sing, preach, or evangelize in order to reach the world outside the church, or even write. (Matthew 10:19-20) "But when they arrest you, do not worry about what to say or how to say it. At that time you will be given what to say, for it will not be you speaking, but the Spirit of your Father speaking through you."

As you grow in your Christian walk and stay close to God in prayer, Bible study, and obedience, He will reveal His will and call for your life by the desires and inspirations He gives you in your heart. (Psalm 20:4) "May He give you the desire of your heart and make all your plans succeed." (Psalm 37:4) "Delight yourself in the Lord and He will give you the desires of your heart."

At your conversion, the moment you asked Jesus into your heart, you were sealed by God and you became a child of God. (Ephesians 1:13-14) "Having believed, you were marked in Him with a seal, the promised Holy Spirit, who is a deposit guaranteeing our inheritance until the redemption of those who are God's possession--to the praise of His glory."

That is awesome to me! Knowing that now, I belong to God. I am His child and as I will always be there to love, protect, and see to all the needs of my son, God will always be there for us. He is the one who anoints us with the Holy Spirit. That anointing and the feeling in your heart that lets you know that God is with you is very comforting. The Creator of the universe loves us all, and with God as our Father, there is nothing impossible for those who believe.

"Everything is possible for him who believes." (Mark 9:23). The purpose of God sealing us is that now we are certain we are God's own. It guarantees our security that we are preserved as a child of God until the day of redemption.

"Now it is God who makes both us and you stand firm in Christ. He anointed us, set His seal of ownership on us, and put His Spirit in our hearts as a deposit, guaranteeing what is to come." (II Corinthians 1:21-22).

We may get down and discouraged from time to time due to the trials that we are going through, but praise God because we are His and He will never let us stay down! He will not let us be harmed.

"They were told not to harm the grass of the earth or any plant or tree, but only those people who did not have the seal of God on their foreheads." (Revelation 9:4).

In your Christian walk, you will have troubles, but rest in the fact that God loves you and will always be with you. Reading His Word will help you to know His promises and the will for your life. Put them into practice. Just like when you go to the doctor when you are sick if He gives you medicine, it can only help you if you take it. The Lord wants to bless you and wants you to grow as a Christian. But if you do not talk with Him and read His Book of Instructions for your life, you will be making mistakes that you could have prevented with a little understanding of the Bible. Read His Word and study it; it will only benefit you. But remember you have to read all of it because it goes together.

"And do not grieve the Holy Spirit of God, with whom you were sealed for the day of redemption." (Ephesians 4:30).

"Do not add to what I command you and do not subtract from it but keep the commands of the Lord your God that I give you." (Deuteronomy 4:2).

"I warn everyone who hears the words of the prophecy of this book: If anyone adds anything to them, God will add to him the plagues described in this book. And if anyone takes words away from this book of prophecy, God will take away from him his share in the tree of life and in the holy city, which are described in this book." (Revelation 22:18-19).

You can't take parts of it to suit your own needs. The whole Bible fits together for our good and our protection, to help us through life; we are to follow all His commands.

"See that you do all I command you; do not add to it or take away from it." (Deuteronomy 12:32).

"Sanctify them by the truth; your Word is truth." (John 17:17).

All of the Bible is true and is all from God to bless us.

"All Scripture is God-breathed and is useful for teaching, rebuking, correcting and training in righteousness, so that the man of God may be thoroughly equipped for every good work." (II Timothy 3:16-17).

The Word of God was given to us to bless us and to help us go through life with all the love and encouragement that God can give us. He did not leave us down here to walk blindly without help.

"Praise the Lord. Blessed is the man who fears the Lord, who finds great delight in His commands." (Psalm 112:1).

"For the Word of God is living and active. Sharper than any double-edged sword, it penetrates even to dividing soul and spirit, joints and marrow; it judges the thoughts and attitudes of the heart." (Hebrews 4:12).

We can put out the Spirit's fire within us if we are not careful.

"Do not put out the Spirit's fire; do not treat prophecies with contempt." (I Thessalonians 5:19).

In staying close to God in prayer and through His Bible we are better equipped with the knowledge we need in order to stay away from the temptations Satan throws our way. God redeemed us in order to bless us and the Bible will help us to learn how to stay close to God and how to grow as Christians.

"He redeemed us in order that the blessing given to Abraham might come to the Gentiles through Christ Jesus so that by faith we might receive the promise of the Spirit." (Galatians 3:14).

Our Heavenly Father loves us so much. No one really knows just how much, but we can take comfort in knowing that He does love us.

"Great is the Lord and most worthy of praise; His greatness no one can fathom." (Psalm 145:3).

20

Rapture

(**I** Chronicles 16:34-35) "Give thanks to the Lord, for He is good; His love endures forever. Cry out, "Save us, O God our Savior; gather us and deliver us from the nations, that we may give thanks to Your holy name, that we may glory in Your praise."

Besides what Jesus did on Calvary to make it possible for our salvation, I think, and I am sure that all Christians will agree, that the 'Rapture,' or the blessed event that gathers us to heaven, is one of the best ways that God shows His love for us.

"They tell how you turned to God from idols to serve the living and true God, and to wait for His Son from heaven, whom He raised from the dead--Jesus, who rescues us from the coming wrath." (I Thessalonians 1:9-10).

Though it has not happened yet, He lets us know in His Word that it will happen. (Isaiah 26:19-21) "But your dead will live; their bodies will rise. You who dwell in the dust, wake up and shout for joy. Your dew is like the dew of the morning; the earth will give birth to her dead. Go, my people, enter your rooms and shut the doors behind you; hide yourselves for a little while until His wrath has passed by. See, the Lord is coming out of His dwelling to punish the people of the earth for their sins. The earth will disclose the bloodshed upon her; she will conceal her slain no longer."

The day we all get to heaven will truly be a day of rejoicing. For there will be no more worry, no more pain and suffering, no more grief and heartaches! We will have peace and joy eternally, praise God!

The word 'Rapture,' is not mentioned in the Bible anywhere. When we as Christians talk about the 'Rapture,' we are talking about the blessed hope of being in heaven with Jesus Christ and the extreme happiness that we will feel when we get there. For in an instant, when the trumpet blows we will be carried away to heaven.

"Gather to Me My consecrated ones, who made a covenant with Me by sacrifice." (Psalm 50:5).

According to Webster's New American Dictionary, the word 'Rapture' means, "the state of being carried away with joy, love, etc.; ecstasy." (Dictionary, 1995)This is exactly what we will feel when we get to heaven. There are verses in the Bible that clearly state that those of us who are still here will be taken to heaven before the seven years of tribulation begin.

"I tell you, on that night two people will be in one bed; one will be taken and the other left. Two women will be grinding grain together; one will be taken and the other left." (Luke 17:34).

In the Gospel of Matthew, Jesus describes how He will gather His church to Him before the seven years of tribulation are ushered in.

"Two men will be in the field; one will be taken and the other left. Two women will be grinding with a hand mill; one will be taken and the other left." (Matthew 24:40-41).

The Lord says that because of the unbelief of the Jews, He turned to the Gentiles to grant them the gift of His salvation.

"Jesus said to them, 'Have you never read in the Scriptures: The stone the builders rejected has become the capstone; the Lord has done this, and it is marvelous in our eyes? Therefore I tell you that the kingdom of God will be taken away from you and given to a people who will produce its fruit. He who falls on this stone will be broken to pieces, but he on whom it falls will be crushed.'" (Matthew 21:42-44)

As Paul and Barnabas were teaching the good news of salvation in Jerusalem, many of the Jews and devout converts to Judaism followed them and told them to continue spreading the word in the grace of God. On the next Sabbath, almost the whole city of Jerusalem gathered to hear them speak.

"When the Jews saw the crowds, they were filled with jealousy and talked abusively against what Paul was saying. Then Paul and Barnabas answered them boldly: 'We had to speak the Word of God to you first. Since you reject it and do not consider yourselves worthy of eternal life, we now turn to the Gentiles. For this is what the Lord has commanded us: 'I have made you a light for the Gentiles, that you may bring salvation to the ends of the earth." (Acts 13:45-47).

God predestined a number of the Gentiles to be saved.

"For those God foreknew He also predestined to be conformed to the likeness of His Son, that He might be the firstborn among many brothers. And those He predestined, He also called; those He called, He also justified; those He justified, He also glorified." (Romans 8:29-30).

When all the Gentiles who are predestined for salvation are saved, He will then turn back to the Jews to save them.

"I do not want you to be ignorant of this mystery, brother, so that you may not be conceited: Israel has experienced a hardening in part until the full number of the Gentiles has come in. And so all Israel will be saved, as it is written: 'The deliverer will come from Zion; He will turn godlessness away from Jacob. And this is My covenant with them when I take away their sins.'" (Romans 11:25-27).

The Jews will be gathered back together, and they will return to the Lord. They will believe in the Lord Jesus Christ and be saved.

"He will raise a banner for the nations and gather the exiles of Israel; He will assemble the scattered people of Judah from the four quarters of the earth." (Isaiah 11:12).

"The ransomed of the Lord will return. They will enter Zion with singing; everlasting joy will crown their heads. Gladness and joy will overtake them, and sorrow and sighing will flee away." (Isaiah 51:11).

Before He turns back to the Jews, He will call His church home first.

"Since you have kept My command to endure patiently, I will also keep you from the hour of trial that is going to come upon the whole world to test those who live on the earth." (Revelation 3:10).

In the Book of Leviticus, the Feast of Trumpets is described here as "a day of rest." They were to gather together to hold a sacred assembly and were not to do any regular work and it was initiated with trumpet blasts. They were to present offerings to the Lord by fire. It was held on the first day of the seventh month, which was Tishri (September-October). As the trumpet blasts of the Feast of Trumpets usher in the Israelites to gather together (Ingathering) to worship the Lord, it will also usher in the seven-year tribulation.

"Listen, I tell you a mystery: We will not all sleep, but we will all be changed--in a flash, in the twinkling of an eye, at the last trumpet. For the trumpet will sound, the dead will be raised imperishable, and we will be changed. For the perishable must clothe itself with the imperishable and the mortal with immortality. When the perishable has been clothed with the imperishable, and the mortal with immortality, then the saying that is written will come true: 'Death has been swallowed up in victory. Where, O death, is your victory? Where, O death, is your sting.' The sting of death is sin, and the power of sin is the law. But, thanks be to God! He gives us the victory through our Lord Jesus Christ." (I Corinthians 15:51-57).

The Israelites have already started being gathered back to Israel. I am sure you have heard if you listen to any Christian TV or radio stations about organizations that are taking donations to help them get back home. This is a fulfillment of the prophecy that states the Gentiles will help bring the Jews back home. It is already happening!

"This is what the Sovereign Lord says: 'See, I will beckon to the Gentiles, I will lift up my banner to the peoples; they will bring your sons in their arms and carry your daughters on their shoulders." (Isaiah 49:22).

When His church is gathered to Him, the Lord will lead the Jews to salvation.

"The Daughter of Babylon is like a threshing floor at the time it is trampled; the time to harvest her will soon come." (Jeremiah 51:33).

Right after the Feast of Trumpets is the Day of Atonement, which is celebrated once a year. It is also in Tishri, the seventh month, and is held on the tenth day. The Day of Atonement is a day to be observed as a community for cleansing of their sins. This is what will happen as the seven years of tribulation are ushered in.

"But Israel will be saved by the Lord with an everlasting salvation; you will never be put to shame or disgraced, to ages everlasting." (Isaiah 45:17).

The hearts of the Jews will be softened to believe the Word of God and they will be cleansed of their sins and be saved.

"Then I heard the number of those who were sealed: 144,000 from all the tribes of Israel." (Revelation 7:4).

The last of the Feasts in the month of Tishri (September-October) is the Feast of Tabernacles. The Feast of Tabernacles starts on the fifteenth day and is celebrated for seven days. This is a celebration of remembrance of their deliverance from Egypt. It is celebrated after the harvest. This is also a prophecy of the harvest of the Gentiles that will be gathered together to the Lord in heaven.

"For the Lord Himself will come down from heaven, with a loud command, with the voice of the archangel and with the trumpet call of God, and the dead in Christ will rise first. After that, we who are still alive and are left will be caught up together with them in the clouds to meet the Lord in the air. And so we will be with the Lord forever." (I Thessalonians 4:16-17).

Not only will it be a harvest for the Gentiles, but also a harvest for the number of Jews that are destined to be saved.

There will be disastrous times for those who are left. The antichrist will set himself up as God.

"Don't let anyone deceive you in any way, for that day will not come until the rebellion occurs and the man of lawlessness is revealed; the man doomed to destruction. He will oppose and will exalt himself over everything that is called God or is worshiped, so that he sets himself up in God's temple, proclaiming himself to be God." (II Thessalonians 2:3-4).

The people who are living in the Tribulation Period have not known hard times like it will be when the antichrist is revealed and takes over the world.

"For then there will be great distress, unequaled again. If those days had not been cut short, no one would survive, but for the sake of the elect, those days will be been shortened. At that time if anyone says to you, 'Look, here is the Christ!' or 'There he is!' do not believe it. For false Christs and false prophets will appear and perform great signs and miracles to deceive even the elect--if that were possible. See, I have told you ahead of time." (Matthew 24:21-25).

The earth and its inhabitants will reap destruction due to their unbelief, rebellion, and wickedness.

"But the day of the Lord will come like a thief. The heavens will disappear with a roar; the elements will be destroyed by fire, and the earth and everything in it will be laid bare." (II Peter 3:10).

Before that happens, God's chosen people who are left here on earth will be gathered up to Him.

"I looked, and there before me was a white cloud, and seated on the cloud was one 'like a Son of Man' with a crown of gold on His head and a sharp sickle in His hand. Then another angel came out of the temple and called in a loud voice to Him who was sitting on the cloud, 'Take your sickle and reap because the time to reap has come, for the harvest of the earth is ripe.' So, He who was seated on the cloud swung His sickle over the earth, and the earth was harvested." (Revelation 14:14-16).

The Lord will judge the living and the dead when He has called all His people home. He will judge everyone in regard to righteousness; those who have believed in the Lord Jesus Christ are the righteousness of God.

"But now a righteousness from God, apart from the law, has been made known, to which the Law and the Prophets testify. This righteousness from God comes through faith in Jesus Christ to all who believe." (Romans 3:21-22).

Those who continue to rebel will suffer the wrath of God for an eternity. In the Book of Genesis, chapters 18 and 19, tell of the destruction of Sodom and Gomorrah. Abraham was very disturbed by this because his nephew, Lot, lived in Sodom. After speaking with the two angels who were sent to destroy the two cities Abraham got the two angels to agree to spare the cities if they found ten righteous people. There was only Lot and his family. They found none other and decided to destroy the city but to save Lot and his family. The angels told them to leave and not to look back. At leaving the city Lot's wife looked back and was turned into a pillar of salt. We are not to look back at our life of sin when we come to the Lord. We are not to love the world or anything of the world: it is full of sinful desires.

"Do not love the world or anything in the world. If anyone loves the world, the love of the Father is not in him. For everything in the world-- the cravings of sinful man, the lust of his eyes and the boasting of what he has and does-- comes not from the Father but from the world. The world and its desires pass away, but the man who does the will of God lives forever." (I John 2:15-17).

This destruction of Sodom and Gomorrah is a symbol of how the world will be destroyed when Jesus returns and of the destruction of all who reject Jesus as Lord and Savior. The ones who receive Him and do the will of God, the Father will inherit eternal life.

"The righteous perish, and no one ponders it in his heart; devout men are taken away, and no one understands that the righteous are taken away to be spared from evil." (Isaiah 57:1).

Thanks be to God! For all who believe and receive Jesus with a sincere heart and not lip service, will be spared the seven horrifying years of Tribulation!

"We give thanks to you, Lord God Almighty, the One who is and who was, because You have taken your great power and have begun to reign. The nations were angry, and Your wrath has come. The time has come for judging the dead, and for rewarding Your servants the prophets and Your saints, and those who reverence Your name, both small and great-- and for destroying those who destroy the earth. Then God's temple in heaven was opened, and within His temple was seen the ark of His covenant. And there came flashes of lightning, rumblings, peals of thunder, and earthquake and a great hailstorm." (Revelation 11:17:19).

No one knows when that time will come; no one knows when the hour and time of their death will be. The only one who does know is the one who created us, our Almighty Father in heaven.

"Now, brothers, about times and dates we do not need to write to you, for you know very well that the day of the Lord will come like a thief in the night." (I Thessalonians 5:1-2).

Living for the Lord is a blessing. He gives you so much peace. You still have trials to go through, but we all do anyway and I would rather go through with the Lord on my side than with Him against me; especially knowing that my time here on earth could be up at any given moment. I for one do not want to take any chances. Living here on earth is hard enough; I sure don't want an eternity in hell as well. As long as the Lord is your Savior, then the 'day of the Lord' should not be a worry to you because you know where you are going.

"Concerning the coming of our Lord Jesus Christ and our being gathered to Him, we ask you brothers, not to become easily unsettled or alarmed by some prophecy, report, or letter supposed to have come from us, saying that the day of the Lord has already come." (II Thessalonians 2:1-2).

When the Lord comes there will not be any doubt. You will know it! Then God will reign forever.

"The seventh angel sounded His trumpet, and there were loud voices in heaven, which said: 'The kingdom of the world has become the kingdom of our Lord and of His Christ, and He will reign forever and ever." (Revelation 11:15).

Satan is doomed and there will be a new heaven and a new earth. (Revelation 20:10) "And the devil, who deceived them, was thrown into the lake of burning sulfur, where the beast and the false prophet had been thrown. They will be tormented day and night forever and ever."

Heaven and earth will be one of peace; there will be no more wars and no more pain.

"Then I saw a new heaven and a new earth, for the first heaven and the first earth had passed away, and there was no longer any sea. I saw the Holy City, the new Jerusalem, coming down out of heaven from God, prepared as a bride beautifully dressed for her husband." (Revelation 21:1-2).

The Lord tells us to be prepared, to be clothed with His righteousness so we will be ready. Are you ready?

"Behold, I come like a thief! Blessed is he who stays awake and keeps his clothes with him, so that he may not go naked and be shamefully exposed." (Revelation 16:15).

We all have this glorious hope of being with Jesus; Satan is fighting a losing battle, for in Christ we have won the victory. We have overcome! (I John 3:2) "Dear friends, now we are children of God, and what will be has not yet been made known. But we know that when He appears we shall be like Him, for we shall see Him as He is."

Our Heavenly Father loves us so much. He has given us all that we need to overcome Satan: Jesus Christ, His One and Only Son, the Holy Spirit, and His Word.

"Be always on the watch, and pray that you may be able to escape all that is about to happen and that you may be able to stand before the Son of Man." (Luke 21:36).

As long as you believe in Jesus and receive Him as your Lord and Savior, His Holy Spirit will guide you through life. He will open the doors of your heart to an understanding of His Word as you read it and put it into practice. This will help you travel down the road of life here on earth victoriously and into the gates of heaven for an eternity of peace.

"Be exalted, O God, above the heavens; let your glory be over all the earth." (Psalm 57:5).

21

Jesus

(John 1:1-2) "In the beginning was the Word, and the Word was with God, and the Word was God. He was with God in the beginning."

The Word is Jesus Christ. Have you ever looked into the face of love? This is the picture that the Word of God radiates as you read it, especially the gospels. When you read it and picture Jesus you see pure love radiated beyond measure. I mentioned this in a previous chapter, but there is so much more to say. Jesus is the reason for all of the blessed ways described in this book that God, the Father shows His love for us. This is truly the best chapter of all, which is why I have saved this for last. He is all of this and more. Jesus is love personified.

"Dear friends let us love one another, for love comes from God." (I John 4:7).

When all hell broke loose, when Satan fell to earth, heaven came down; Jesus.

"The Word became flesh and made His dwelling among us." (John 1:14).

The world was formless and void before God spoke it into being.

"In the beginning, God created the heavens and the earth. Now the earth was formless and empty, darkness was over the surface of the deep, and the Spirit of God was hovering over the waters. And God said, 'Let there be light', and there was light. God saw that the light was good, and He separated the light from the darkness." (Genesis 1:1-4).

Jesus is that light and when His light enters your heart, all darkness has to go. It has to flee. When you come into a dark room and flip the light switch on, the darkness leaves. So it is with your heart. There is a newness and fullness of life that you never experienced before and never want to part from now that you know it.

"I am the light of the world. Whoever follows Me will never walk in darkness, but will have the light of life." (John 8:12).

Everyone has a God-shaped hole in his or her heart that only God can fill. When Christ fills your heart, He makes you whole; you have His fullness and the fullness of God within you through Jesus Christ.

"For in Christ all the fullness of the Deity lives in bodily form, and you have been given fullness in Christ, who is the head over every power and authority." (Colossians 2:9-10).

He would not create us to fill that hole with anything else but Him. As you believe in Jesus and receive Him you become a child of God. You have a new family! Rejoice! The person of Jesus brings you love and relationship; the principles of Jesus bring prosperity in spirit, emotions, mind, relationships, finances, and life.

"The thief comes to steal, and kill and destroy; I have come that they may have life, and have it to the full." (John 10:10).

Life has a way of handing you some very difficult and heavy loads to bear. We were given free will. God wants us to love Him freely; He gives us the choice and due to that some people make some very bad choices. We suffer due to that or from the bad choices that we ourselves have made. Then one day you finally wake up and realize that you need Jesus and you cannot do this life thing without Him. You realize that you need help and you need a Savior and Lord. You realize that there is a Heaven and a Hell and if you do not repent and receive Him as Lord you could die and go that hell. I did this, not realizing from all the pain that I suffered through, that I was not only seeking a Savior but also a deliverer.

This in itself is not bad; that is what Jesus is. But He is so much more. It took losing so much, my son and my parents, separation from my husband, and the only son that I had left moving out of state. I was all alone, and it was then that, through the revelation of God and many prayers asking God. "who are You to me, and when will I have someone to love me?" that I realized I had that love all along. Through watching a movie about people separating Jesus from God's commandments, God showed me that I had done the same thing. I started questioning myself and realized I was searching for deliverance from all the pain I had felt, but not the deliverer: Jesus. I had the love I needed all along. When I realized that Jesus is in me and He is the love that I had been seeking all along I burst into tears. Tears of joy! I felt something in me wake up. I felt a newness inside and was full of great joy!

"Therefore, if anyone is in Christ, he is a new creation; the old has gone, the new has come!" (II Corinthians 5:17).

I had love in me! I had been searching for something that I had all along, I just did not know it. That is how Satan keeps you down; he blinds your eyes from the truth.

"The god of this age has blinded the minds of unbelievers so that they cannot see the light of the gospel of the glory of Christ, who is the image of God." (II Corinthians 4:4).

Once your eyes are opened to it you are truly free. I was finally free and all the pain that I had felt for so long seemed to just disappear.

"So, if the Son sets you free, you will be free indeed." (John 8:36).

I was truly happy. Jesus became so real to me at that moment, as if for the very first time. I had love inside me. You look at Jesus and you see love. The love of God in Christ Jesus completes you.

"No one has ever seen God; but if we love one another, God lives in us and His love is made complete in us." (I John 4:12).

Until we have His perfect love living within us through Jesus we will always have a God-shaped hole in our hearts. It is made for God's love and the searching will continue until we fill it. Nothing else will fit or give you the contentment and the peace that having the Holy Spirit of Jesus Christ gives when He is living within your heart.

When David went to King Saul to offer his service in going up against

Goliath and fighting him to save the people, Saul gave him his armor to wear. It did not fit, and nor will any other god that we may chase after fit the God hole in our hearts. Only the One true God and Father, Creator of Heaven and earth will fit into that hole through the Holy Spirit of our Lord and Savior Jesus Christ. My circumstances had not changed but I had never felt so happy before and I wanted to shout it to the world! The love of Jesus tells you that you belong; it tells you that you matter and that you are worth something. Jesus is the love of God so great for mankind that He died for us all.

"This is how we know what love is: Jesus Christ laid down His life for us. And we ought to lay down our lives for our brothers. If anyone has material possessions and sees his brother in need but has no pity on him, how can the love of God be in him?" (I John 3:16-17).

Jesus is God's perfect love; His Mercy Seat, which is why, when you receive Him into your heart, all that which was keeping a battle going on inside of you, filling your heart with pain, fear, loneliness, and worthlessness, must leave.

"There is no fear in love. But perfect love drives out fear because fear has to do with punishment. The one who fears is not made perfect in love." (I John 4:18).

This is because Jesus took our punishment for us. He already paid the price; if you have not truly received Him then truly loving unconditionally as He does will come hard for you. His love within us compels us to love others. He is perfect love and we cannot help but to love others.

"I ask that we love one another. And this is love: that we walk in obedience to His commands. As you have heard from the beginning, His command is that you walk in love." (II John: 5-6).

If Jesus is love and we know that He is, His sacrifices prove it, and love covers a multitude of sins, then with the Holy Spirit of Jesus in us, His love covers all our sins.

"Above all, love each other deeply because love covers over a multitude of sins." (I Peter 4:8).

As well, His love in us should help us to overlook the sins of others. He tells us to clothe ourselves with Jesus.

"Rather clothe yourselves with the Lord Jesus Christ, and do not think about how to gratify the desires of the sinful nature." (Romans 13:14).

The love of Jesus covering us and completing us helps us to do all things.

"I can do everything through Him who gives me strength." (Philippians 4:13).

With His love and strength within you, forgiving others and looking past their faults, and the things they do to offend you will be easy to do as you depend on Jesus to love people through you, "with God all things are possible."

If you have repented of your sins sincerely and asked Jesus into your heart then His overwhelming love lives in you and covers you. When God looks at you He sees the blood of His sinless Son covering you. He sees you righteous through Jesus. He sees His perfect love in you.

"Don't be deceived, my dear brothers. Every good and perfect gift is from above, coming down from the Father of the heavenly lights, who does not change like the shifting shadows." (James 1:16-17).

He has clothed you with salvation and love.

"For He has clothed me with garments of salvation and arrayed me in a robe of righteousness." (Isaiah 61:10).

When God the Father looks down on you, does He see Jesus portrayed in you and your life? Has His perfect love filled your heart? It is not too late. His perfect love fills us and completes us in every way.

"And God placed all things under His feet and appointed Him to be head over everything for the church, which is His body, the fullness of Him who fills everything in every way." (Ephesians 1:22-23).

You can love completely and walk in that love daily.

"Dear friends, since God so loved us, we also ought to love one another. No one has ever seen God; but if we love one another, God lives in us and His love is made complete in us." (I John 4:11-12).

It is a choice. It is part of that "dying to self" process that we all have to walk in daily as long as we are here on earth. With the love of Jesus, you can do it.

"Anyone who claims to be in the light but hates his brother is still in the darkness. Whoever loves his brother lives in the light, and there is nothing in him to make him stumble." (I John 2:9-10).

Jesus came as a servant, loving, healing, dying, and forgiving. He set the example for us to follow.

"I have set you an example that you should do as I have done for you." (John 13:15).

"But God demonstrates His own love for us in this: While we were still sinners, Christ died for us." (Romans 5:8).

Jesus glorified the Father. He walked in love and died in love for us. Do you? How do you treat the person who stops you for help in your busy day? Do you remember how Jesus came from the glory of heaven to live as a servant, suffer, and die on the cross in pure agony for you? Do you remember that, and in the love of God help them? Or do you snap at them and tell them you don't have time?

"To this you were called, because Christ suffered for you, leaving you an example that you should follow in His steps." (I Peter 2:21).

Just because you may have said the words, "Jesus come into my heart," is it really true? If you did not mean it then you need to examine your heart.

"Not everyone who says to Me, 'Lord, Lord,' will enter the kingdom of heaven, but only he who does the will of My Father who is in heaven." (Matthew 7:21).

Romans 10:9-10 says that if you believe in your heart and confess you are saved. If you truly believed in your heart and repent of your sins, His love will compel you to live His love out loud every day. Love must be sincere.

"Let us draw near to God with a sincere heart in full assurance of faith." (Hebrews 10:22).

Have you asked Jesus to forgive you yet you hold a grudge in your heart every time someone wrongs you?

"For if you forgive men when they sin against you, your heavenly Father will also forgive you. But if you do not forgive men their sins, your Father will not forgive your sins." (Matthew 6:14-15).

Do you read the Bible and go to church and think that will get you into heaven? Think again. We must live it and let our daily lives be worship unto God.

"Do not merely listen to the word, and so deceive yourselves. Do what it says." (James 1:22).

If you do not put your faith in Jesus to work in you and live it out daily, it is dead faith.

"If one of you says to him, 'Go, I wish you well; keep warm and well fed,' but does nothing about his physical needs, what good is it? In the same way, faith by itself, if it is not accompanied by action, is dead. But someone will say, 'You have faith; I have deeds.' Show me your faith without deeds, and I will show you my faith by what I do. You believe that there is one God. Good! Even the demons believe that and shudder." (James 2:16-19).

As you walk in the love of Jesus daily, not only witnessing, which we are called to do, but also by living it, your daily life can be a testimony in itself. People will know and see Jesus in you as you walk in His love. You may be the only "Jesus" they see.

"A new command I give you: Love one another. As I have loved you, so you must love one another. By this all men will know that you are My disciples if you love one another." (John 13:34-35).

So, ask yourself daily, have I reflected Jesus today?

"As water reflects a face, so a man's heart reflects the man." (Proverbs 27:19).

When you finally open your heart up to the wonders of the love of God, Jesus Christ, it is the most beautiful thing in the entire world. As you let Him love through you, everything and everyone will seem different to you. Let Jesus teach you and show you who He really is and what it truly means to love.

"Show me Your ways, O Lord, teach me Your paths; guide me in Your truth and teach me, for you are God my Savior, and my hope is in You all day long." (Psalm 25:4-5).

Your heart will feel light and free. You will feel as if you were on top of the world. You will not just love people as you see them from the outside, looking at who you see them to be and how they act toward you, but you will love as Jesus does. He loves from the inside out! He loves the very heart of who we are. Where would we all be if God chose to love us for our actions?

"All of us have become like one who is unclean, and all our righteous acts are like filthy rags." (Isaiah 64:6).

God sees our hearts.

"The lamp of the Lord searches the spirit of a man; it searches out his inmost being." (Proverbs 20:27).

We can love that way because His love is in us. His ability to love others is in us and will give us that ability to love others in the same way, as we let Him love through us. We just have to yield to His Spirit and obey.

We are not to love people by how they treat us, by their brittle actions and their mean and unkind words, but despite them. This is how He loves us.

"If you love those who love you, what reward will you get? Are not even the tax collectors doing that? And if you greet only your brothers, what are you doing more than others? Do not even pagans do that?" (Matthew 5:46-47).

You need to ask yourself who or what caused them so much hurt to turn their heart so hard and brittle. Say for instance you are walking in the park. It is a beautiful day and very peaceful. Then up ahead as you walk you see a woman sitting on a park bench with her head cupped in her hands as she cries profusely. You see a man standing over her pointing his finger at her and yelling mean things at her, not caring about who hears by the tone of his voice. There is fury in his voice and his eyes. Who do you want to reach out and hug? Our human nature wants to hug the woman. But not so with God. He wants to hug them both. That is because He loves from the inside out; He sees their heart.

"All a man's ways seem right to him but the Lord weighs the heart." (Proverbs 21:2).

The woman has enough heart in her that she still feels the emotion to cry, and while she needs compassion, and everyone will reap the consequences for their actions, this does not change the love of God. His love is unconditional. The man has had so much hurt heaped on him through his life that his heart has turned so hard, so brittle and mean, that he does not have any compassion left in him or he would not have humiliated the woman in public like he did. God's love can soften a heart like that. Jesus came into the world to save it; not condemn it.

"For God so loved the world that He gave His One and Only Son, that whoever believes in Him shall not perish but have eternal life. For God did not send His Son into the world to condemn the world, but to save the world through Him." (John 3:16-17).

He set the example; He loved us first. Then, as we believe, we love Him back.

"We love because He first loved us." (I John 4:19).

Love covers all sin, all wrongdoing. In His example, we are to love others to Christ. As He loves us first, we are to let the love of God love them through us. It will melt the hardest of hearts. Jesus offers us love and a family. In loving, believing, and receiving Him, we become part of the family of God.

"Yet to all who received Him, to those who believe in His name, He gave the right to become children of God." (John 1:12).

Jesus offers life eternally, love, self-worth, wholeness, and healing. Satan causes eternal death, hate, bitterness, unforgiveness, selfishness, revenge, depression, suicide, murder, and the list goes on. He keeps your heart heavy, angry, and depressed. He causes self-hatred. Jesus says that you are "the righteousness of God in Christ Jesus." Satan accuses you of your wrongdoings and causes others to never forget.

"For the accuser of our brothers, who accuses them before our God day and night, has been hurled down." (Revelation 12:10).

Jesus forgets and helps us to do the same for others who have wronged us.

"For I will forgive their wickedness and will remember their sins no more." (Hebrews 8:12).

So, which way is better? God rains on the just and the unjust.

"He causes His sun to rise on the evil and the good and sends rain on the righteous and the unrighteous." (Matthew 5:45).

He created all people and watches over all people.

"The eyes of the Lord are everywhere, keeping watch on the wicked and the good." (Proverbs 15:3).

He sent Jesus to die for all people. It is their choice to receive Him or not, but it is their choice and not ours. Just as God sends rain to soften the hard ground, the love of Jesus can soften the hardest of hearts; a heart that has been hurt so badly and for so long that it has turned hard, brittle, and mean.

"I will give you a new heart and put a new spirit in you; I will remove from you your heart of stone and give you a heart of flesh." (Ezekiel 36:26).

Paul prayed in (Ephesians 1:18) "I pray also that the eyes of your heart may be enlightened in order that you may know the hope to which He has called you, the riches of His glorious inheritance in the saints and His incomparably great power for us who believe."

He prayed this because love does not look with the eyes-- the flesh but with the heart. This is where Jesus resides.

Up to now, we have talked about how God shows His love for us. Giving us Jesus is one of those ways. We have talked about how His love completes us and saves us, but now let's talk about some of the different facets of His love. What makes the love of Jesus what it is? There are many facets of His love.

"Love is patient, love is kind. It does not envy, it does not boast, it is not proud. It is not rude, it is not self-seeking, it is not easily angered, and it keeps no record of wrongs. Love does not delight in evil but rejoices with the truth. It always protects, always trusts, always hopes, and always perseveres. Love never fails." (I Corinthians 13:4-8).

Here are some of them. The first is His unconditional love, which is an *agape* love and only comes from God.

"I have loved you with an everlasting love; I have drawn you with loving-kindness." (Jeremiah 31:3).

He loved us first, while we were sinners, not after He cleaned us up.

He loves us because of who we are, because we are His; not because of what we do.

An *agape love* loves us despite what we do; it is a love that loves freely. His love will birth the fruit of the Spirit within us. With the unconditional love of Jesus within you, you cannot help but love people, want to do for them, and be kind to them. There is nothing that can make the Lord not love us. The *agape* love that God has for mankind has no conditions. He loves us even while we are far away from Him spiritually. The Lord Jesus also had a *phileo* love. This is a brotherly love. This is a caring love.

Moses was a friend of God.

"The Lord would speak to Moses face to face, as a man speaks with his friend." (Exodus 33:11).

He loved the disciples as friends, as family. John 1:12 says, "Yet to all who received Him, to those who believed in His name, He gave the right to become children of God."

If we are God's children, then we are all brothers and sisters in Christ.

"A man of many companions may come to ruin, but there is a friend who sticks closer than a brother." (Proverbs 18:24).

He prayed to the Father in John 17:24 "Father, I want those you have given Me to be with Me where I am, and to see My glory, the glory You have given Me because You loved Me before the creation of the world."

Our Lord also has an *eros* love. An *eros* love is an intimate love. This is the kind of love that a man and a woman have for each other. Our Lord loves us that way. He loves every one of us intimately. Each of us can have a personal relationship with Jesus. The closer we draw to Him the closer He comes to us.

"Submit yourselves, then, to God. Resist the devil, and he will flee from you. Come near to God and He will come near to you." (James 4:7-8).

It is up to you and how devoted you choose to be to Him. Abraham had abundant faith as he set out to a new country at God's command, and again as he offered up his only son to God. Moses was humble and reverent, David had a heart of worship, Joseph was faithful through all he went through, Job persevered; he truly possessed long-suffering. Paul yielded completely to the Holy Spirit and was truly on fire; he preached the Word of God boldly. He wrote 13 of the 27 books of the New Testament. You can possess all these qualities. It is up to you and how devoted, teachable, and submissive you want to be. He has plans for each of us and if we were the only ones on earth He would have still died for us.

"I tell you that in the same way, there will be more rejoicing in heaven over one sinner who repents than over ninety-nine righteous persons who do not need to repent." (Luke 15:7).

He has plans for each of us.

"For I know the plans I have for you, declares the Lord, plans to prosper you and not to harm you, plans to give you hope and a future." (Jeremiah 29:11).

When we are taken captive to sin, when we backslide, God weeps. He longs to bless us but out of His great love, our Heavenly Father is one of covenant and a Father. When we do something wrong, true love will discipline us. The previous verse is one of many that state how God longs to bless us.

In John, Chapter 11, as Lazarus took deathly sick, He was told in verse 3, "Lord, the one you love is sick," and in verses 35-36 when He saw the great sorrow of those that loved Lazarus when he died it says, "Jesus wept. Then the Jews said, 'See how He loved him!'"

This is up close and personal. You weep over those you are truly intimate with.

"But if you do not listen, I will weep in secret because of your pride; My eyes will weep bitterly, overflowing with tears, because the Lord's flock will be taken captive." (Jeremiah 13:17).

Another facet of His love is patience. Love endures all; it is long-suffering. God is patient with us and with all of the many mistakes we make along the way to where He wants us to end up. We just need to keep walking in His presence daily.

"He is patient with you, not wanting anyone to perish, but everyone to come to repentance." (II Peter 3:19).

He loves us when we are bitter, angry, and sad, and living out our own will. That leads to another facet of His love; mercy. His love shows us mercy. Mercy is not earned; it is given.

"But when the kindness and love of God our Savior appeared, He saved us, not because of righteous things we had done, but because of His mercy. He saved us through the washing of rebirth and renewal by the Holy Spirit, whom He poured out on us generously through Jesus Christ our Savior, so that, having been justified by His grace, we might become heirs having the hope of eternal life." (Titus 3:4-7).

We all need God's mercy and want it from others. "Give and it will be given unto you." The people you do not want to show it to are the ones who need it the most. That includes all of us; mankind!

"For all have sinned and fall short of the glory of God." (Romans 3:23).

Joseph had good reason to despise his brothers for what they did to him, yet when they needed food he chose to show mercy to them and forgive. For that, the whole family was restored and put back together better than it was before. Where there once was jealousy, love replaced it. Where would we all be if not for the grace and mercy of God? Do you return His great mercy to others? How can you expect God to show you mercy if you do not show it to others?

"Therefore, if you are offering your gift at the altar and there remember that your brother has something against you; leave your gift there in front of the altar. First, go and be reconciled to your brother, then come and offer your gift." (Matthew 5:23-24).

This leads us to yet another facet of His love; forgiveness. Love never holds on to offenses. It always forgives and forgets as Jesus forgives us.

"Praise the Lord, O my soul, and forget not all His benefits--who forgives all your sins and heals all your diseases." (Psalm 103:2-3).

We can always go to the Father and repent and ask forgiveness.

"If we claim to be without sin, we deceive ourselves and the truth is not in us. If we confess our sins, He is faithful and just and will forgive us our sins and purify us from all unrighteousness." (I John 1:8-9).

He remembers that we are but flesh and the flesh is weak.

"As a Father has compassion on his children, so the Lord has compassion on those who fear Him; for He knows how we are formed, He remembers that we are dust." (Psalm 103:13-14).

God knows and understands our hearts. He knows that perfection will not come to us until we receive our glorified bodies in heaven. This leads to another facet of the love of Jesus; understanding. He knows our hearts and He knows when we are sad and the emotions we battle from trials that we have been through. He knows the things that cause us or have caused us great pain.

"Great is our Lord and mighty in power; His understanding has no limit." (Psalm 147:5).

Another facet of His love is compassion. Since He knows our hearts whether hardhearted or very loving, He knows what drives our actions. Even the meanest person you could imagine has a heart inside that has been hurt at one point or another in his life. The Lord knows it and how to heal it.

"Because of the Lord's great love, we are not consumed, for His compassions never fail. They are new every morning; great is your faithfulness." (Lamentations 3:22-23).

The compassion of the Lord is what compelled Him to heal.

"A man with leprosy came to Him and begged him on his knees, 'If you are willing, you can make me clean.' Filled with compassion, Jesus reached out His hand and touched the man. 'I am willing,' He said. 'Be clean." Immediately the leprosy left him and he was cured." (Mark 1:40-42).

His compassion fed the 5000 as He also taught them. His compassion supplies our needs as well.

"He grants peace to your borders and satisfies you with the finest of wheat." (Psalm 147:14).

The compassion and love of Jesus compel Him to save us, forgive us, heal us, deliver us, protect us, comfort us, and supply all our needs.

Jesus draws people to Himself through compassion and love, not criticism and humiliation. This leads us to yet another facet of His love: an edifying love.

"From Him, the whole body, joined and held together by every supporting ligament, grows and builds itself up in love, as each part does its work." (Ephesians 4:16).

An edifying love tells you that you are worth something. It tells you that you are valuable. This kind of love wants to make someone feel good about himself or herself and make them happy. An edifying love is not selfish or self-seeking. It longs to do for others, to give of self for the good of others. It places others' needs before their own.

"Are not two sparrows sold for a penny? Yet not one of them will fall to the ground apart from the will of your Father. And even the very hairs of your head are all numbered. So don't be afraid, you are worth more than many sparrows." (Matthew 10:29-31).

You are worth so much that He died for you. Another facet of His love is faithfulness. The love of Jesus is faithful. Jesus never gave up; He did not abandon the cross, He carried it.

"The Lord is faithful to all His promises and loving to all He has made." (Psalm 145:13).

On Christ you can always depend; the seeds of faith that you plant and the trust in Jesus that you have is the electric wiring that connects to God's power. Your prayers will be answered. "He will never fail or forsake you." A farmer does not plant seeds one day and expects to harvest them the very next day. God is faithful; if you believe and wait in trust and thanksgiving then God will bring it to pass.

"Not one of the Lord's good promises to the house of Israel failed; every one was fulfilled." (Joshua 21:45).

Another facet of His love is humility. Jesus did not come wearing a crown; He wore a cross on His shoulders and hung on it.

"Your attitude should be the same as that of Christ Jesus: Who being in very nature God; did not consider equality with God something to be grasped, but made Himself nothing, taking the very nature of a servant, being made in human likeness. And being found in appearance as a man, He humbled Himself and became obedient to death even death on a cross!" (Philippians 2: 5-8).

He came dressed as a servant.

"For you know the grace of our Lord Jesus Christ that though He was rich, yet for your sake He became poor so that you through His poverty might become rich." (II Corinthians 8:9).

The love of Jesus does not exalt self; it exalts others.

"Do nothing out of selfish ambition or vain conceit, but in humility consider others better than yourselves." (Philippians 2:3)

He humbled Himself and God raised Him up.

"Therefore God exalted Him to the highest place and gave Him the name that is above every name." (Philippians 2:9).

Another facet of His love is a servant love. When you truly love someone you want to bless them and do for them. Not to receive something in return, but because you love them with all your heart, and blessing them blesses you.

"Just as the Son of Man did not come to be served, but to serve, and to give His life as a ransom for many." (Matthew 20:28).

Another facet of His love is obedience. Love does what is right and obeys God out of reverence for Him.

"During the days of Jesus' life on earth, He offered up prayers and petitions with loud cries and tears to the One who could save Him from death, and He was heard because of His reverent submission. Although He was a Son, He learned obedience from what He suffered and, once made perfect, He became the source of eternal salvation for all who obey Him and was designated by God to be high priest in the order of Melchizedek." (Hebrews 5:7-10).

When you obey God and His commands you cannot help but treat others with love. By our faith in Him, that love in return compels us to obey God.

"Through Him and for His name's sake, we received grace and apostleship to call people from among all the Gentiles to the obedience that comes from faith." (Romans 1:5).

The love of God in Jesus always did what the Father asked and He was raised from the dead. Our love and faith in Him raises our hearts to life as well.

"But if Christ is in you, your body is dead because of sin, yet your spirit is alive because of righteousness. And if the Spirit of Him who raised Jesus from the dead is living in you, He who raised Christ from the dead will also give life to your mortal bodies through His Spirit, who lives in you." (Romans 8:10-11).

The last one is a sacrificial love. In love, Jesus gave His life for us that we may be saved.

"Greater love has no one than this, that he lay down his life for his friends." (John 15:13).

Jesus prayed earnestly in the garden as He felt the weight of what He was about to do, and yet He still chose to give His life for us.

"And being in anguish, He prayed more earnestly, and His sweat was like drops of blood falling to the ground." (Luke 22:44).

Through the love and obedience of Jesus Christ, we have life everlasting, and all we need here on earth to make it through every trial as we yield our soul, our life, and our spirits unto Him.

"I am the resurrection and the life. He who believes in Me will live, even though he dies, and whoever lives and believes in Me will never die. Do you believe this?" (John 11:25-26).

Do you truly believe in Jesus and the overwhelming love He has for mankind? How many people do you know that would take on the punishment that Jesus took for you? How many people do you know that would die for you? Have you truly accepted His love? Or will you be one that will cause Him to weep bitterly? It is that *eros* love that He has for each of us that causes Him to weep when by our own actions we separate ourselves from Him. Have you ever been separated from someone that you love? Did you not weep for them because you missed them so much? Jesus loves us so much, even when we choose a path that separates us from Him. Whether for a period of time here on earth or for eternity, He feels the pain of separation just like you and me, and He weeps bitterly. Do you want to be the reason for the tears that flow from our Master's face?

Jesus is everything we need. He is our Master, our Lord, King of Kings, our Prince of Peace, Lion of the tribe of Judah, our Messiah, Immanuel, Wonderful Counselor, Strongtower, A Friend that sticks closer than a brother, Mighty God, Everlasting Father, Lamb of God our Savior. The love of God does not compare to anything else in all creation nor can anything separate us from it.

"Who shall separate us from the love of Christ? Shall trouble or hardship or persecution or famine or nakedness or danger or sword? As it is written: 'For your sake, we face death all day long; we are considered a sheep to be slaughtered.' No, in all these things we are more than conquerors through Him who loved us. For I am convinced that neither death nor life, neither angels nor demons, neither the present nor the future, nor any powers, neither height nor depth nor anything else in all creation will be able to separate us from the love of God that is in Christ Jesus our Lord." (Romans 8:35-39).

Nothing else can fill us the way He does, love us the way He loves us, or save us. His names say it all. Here are a few of His names:

Jehovah--Self-existent, I Am that I Am-whatever we need is who He is.
Elohim--Strong one -He is all-powerful. No one or nothing is mightier!
Adonai-Lord- He is God, Lord He should be Lord over everything
El Elyon--Most High God
El Olam--Everlasting God
El Shaddai--Almighty God
El Roi--The Strong One
Yahweh--I am the One; Isarael's Covenant God
Jehovah Jireh--The Lord Provides
Jehovah Nissi--The Lord is my Banner
Jehovah Shalom--The Lord is Peace
Jehovah Raah/Rohi--The Lord is my Shepherd

Jehovah Rophe--The Lord Heals

Jehovah Shammah--The Lord who is Present

Jehovah Tsidkenu--The Lord our Righteousness

Jehovah Mekadesh--The Lord your Sanctifier

Jehovah Sabbaoth--The Lord of Hosts

Jehovah El Gmolah--The Lord God of Recompense

Jehovah Nakeh--The Lord who Smites

Jehovah Ezer--The Lord our Helper

Our God is Omniscient, Omnipresent, and Omnipotent; meaning all-knowing, everywhere, and all-powerful. Is He your God? After reading this book about how He shows His love to you, doesn't that make you want to remedy the lack of Him in your heart if He is not your God? Most of all, read the best love story ever written: the Bible.

I pray for every one of you "that you, being rooted and established in love, may have power, together with all the saints, to grasp how wide and long and high and deep is the love of Christ, and know this love that surpasses knowledge--that you may be filled to the measure of all the fullness of God." (Ephesians 3:17-19).

Epilogue

God loves us so much that we can never truly comprehend just how much. He loves us no matter what. We fail and forsake Him so many times as we travel down life's highway, but God stays faithful to us and He still loves us just as much as when we were first conceived. That is truly awesome! Our human emotions can't really let us comprehend this because of the many emotions we deal with. God is spirit and God is love. Through His love, He created us, and a plan to keep us with Him through eternity.

We must believe and receive His One and Only Son, Jesus Christ; the atonement for our sins and the source of our love, strength, and faith within our souls. As long as you believe God exists and receive Jesus into your heart, He will be with you through all your good and bad times. He is your strength that will keep you going through each trial. Trust Him. He loves you and will protect you. He shows His love for us daily in so many ways. He gives so much more than we could ever begin to give Him. All He wants is for us to love Him, trust Him, and obey Him. (Deuteronomy 10:12-13) "And now, O Israel, what does the Lord your God ask of you but to fear the Lord your God, to walk in all His ways, to love Him, to serve the Lord you God with all your heart and with all your soul, and to observe the Lord's commands and decrees that I am giving you today for your own good?" When you think of it in that way, and the high price He paid to ensure our eternal salvation, loving Him should be easy.

God is love, God is holy, and He has higher plans for us for when we get to heaven. (Isaiah 55:8-9) "For My thoughts are not your thoughts, neither are your ways My ways,' declares the Lord. 'As the heavens are higher than the earth, so are My ways higher than your ways and My thoughts than your thoughts." Life is just how God molds us into the people He wants us to be. (Colossians 2:17) "These are a shadow of the things that were to come; the reality, however, is found in Christ." If you have never received Jesus into your heart, then recite the prayer on the following page. It will be the best decision you have ever made!

Other Books by Sandra (Lott) Smith

Adult Books

Jeremy's Journey
Safe In Papa's Hands
Her Final Curtain
Deep Waters Within
Deep Waters Rage: Sequel to Deep Waters Within
My Father's Eyes: Seeing Yourself Through The Eyes of Love
Hannah: From Barren to Blossom
Ride the Wind
An Eagle's Flight
A Princess in Waiting
The Princess in the Harlot
Step By Step Into A Deeper Walk In Christ
I'm Saved! Where Do I Go From Here?
The Day Hope Was Born: God's Gift of Love
The Holy Spirit and the Baptism of the Holy Spirit
Repairing Broken Walls: Restoring Joy & Peace-The Book
Repairing Broken Walls: Restoring Joy & Peace-The Study Guide
Jewels From the Word & Manna For the Soul
Captivated By God's Love: Poems From the Heart
You've Got This: Learning To Let Go
I'm Saved! What Next? Beginning Your Walk In Christ
The Father He Never Knew He Needed
In the Garden with Jesus
Princess Anastasia & the Kingdom of Divulgence

Children's Books

The Sheep That Went Astray
Naomi's Joy
Molly's Journey to Forgiveness
Tim & Gerald Ray Series: The Wind Has a Voice
Tim & Gerald Ray Series: How Did He Get in There?
Tim & Gerald Ray Series: A Light in the Sky
Tim & Gerald Ray Series: Let's Go Swimming
Tim & Gerald Ray Series: Blowing in the Wind
Tim & Gerald Ray Series: Summer on Grandma's Farm
Sassy Goes Exploring

Special Invitation

I cannot close this book without giving you the awesome privilege of becoming a child of God, a chance to have every wrong made right and every sin washed away. If you have never asked Jesus into your heart, or maybe you did but you were never sincere, please pray the prayer on the pages following. It will be the best thing you have ever done.

After you do this, find a good Church to go to if you do not have one already. Fellowshipping with other Christians will help you on your new walk in Christ. It is also a place to worship God and learn more about Him. Also, tell someone! You must confess! This should be the happiest day of your life because you now know that your eternal home is in heaven! I think that is the best life insurance anyone can have, and it is free!

(Romans 10:9-10) "That if you confess with your mouth, 'Jesus is Lord,' and believe in your heart that God raised Him from the dead, you will be saved. For it is with your heart that you believe and are justified, and it is with your mouth that you confess and are saved."

Congratulations and welcome to the family of God!

God Loves You!

(Jeremiah. 31:3) "I have loved you with an everlasting love; I have drawn you with loving-kindness."

I Timothy 2:3-4 "God our Savior, who wants all men to be saved and to come to the knowledge of the truth."

He will not knock on the door of your heart forever. Will you let Him in?

Revelation 3:20 "Here I am! I stand at the door and knock. If anyone hears My voice and opens the door, I will come in and eat with him, and he with Me."

Jesus is the only way to God.
John 14:6 "I am the way, the truth, and the life. No one comes to the Father except through Me."

John 3:3 "I tell you the truth, no one can see the kingdom of God unless he is born again."

And you must make Him Lord of your life.
Matthew 6:24 "No one can serve two masters."
Matthew 7:21 "Not everyone who says to Me, 'Lord, Lord', will enter the kingdom of heaven, but only he who does the will of My Father who is in heaven."

We must leave our old ways behind.
Mark 3:25 "If a house is divided against itself, that house cannot stand."

You can't live according to the flesh and desires of the sinful nature and expect to have Jesus in your heart. He is holy. He is love. Love and Hate cannot exist together.

Ephesians 4:22-24 "You were taught, with regard to your former way of life, to put off your old self, which is being corrupted by its deceitful desires; to be made new in the attitude of your minds; and to put on the new self, created to be like God in true righteousness and holiness."

God gives you the ability to do His will. He knows it is hard.
Philippians 4:13 "I can do everything through Him who gives me strength."

Romans 3:23 "For all have sinned and fall short of the glory of God."

I John 1:9 "If we confess our sins, He is faithful and just and will forgive us our sins and purify us from all unrighteousness."

John 1:12 "Yet to all who received Him, to those who believed in His name, He gave the right to become children of God."

Romans 10:10 "For it is with your heart that you believe and are justified, and it is with your mouth that you confess and are saved."

Then after you confess and ask forgiveness and receive Jesus into your heart, you must testify (tell someone) and be baptized. In this, God is glorified, and others might be saved by your example.

II Timothy 1:8 "So do not be ashamed to testify about our Lord"

I Peter 3:21 "And this water symbolizes baptism that now saves you also- not the removal of dirt from the body but the pledge of a good conscience toward God. It saves you by the resurrection of Jesus Christ."

Invitation to Salvation Prayer

Dear Almighty Father in heaven, I know that I am a sinner and I ask your forgiveness of all my sins. I want to make You the Lord of my life and I want to serve You all the days of my life. I believe that Jesus Christ died on the cross for my sins.

Thank you so much for loving me, and waiting for me to come to the knowledge of the truth!

Thank you for my salvation. Please help me and guide me in learning your Word so I can be a light to the world.

Please, Jesus, come into my heart and baptize me with your Holy Spirit.

I thank You and praise Your Holy Name and ask all this in the name of Jesus Christ our Lord. Amen.

Sandra (Lott) Smith was born and raised in San Antonio, Texas, with one sister and two brothers. Sandra loves the mountains, making candles, and jewelry. She is the author of Jeremy's Journey, Deep Waters Within, A Princess in Waiting, Ride the Wind, and more. She has also written children's such as, The Wind Has a Voice and How Did He Get in There, Molly's Journey to Forgiveness, and more. She has written over 38 books to date and began writing poetry as soon as she was saved in June 1998. The Lord gave her, her first book to write right after her son was killed. Writing was not something she sought out. She poured her heart into time spent with the Lord in order to allow Him to heal her heart and the name of her first book was birthed in her spirit along with the chapters and what it was to be about during a devotion time. It was called: God's Love; ironically enough, with all that she was going through, God's love was exactly what she needed.

She is passionate about studying the Bible. She has taught Sunday school, and Bible Study Groups, assists in preaching in her present church, and served in the Celebrate Recovery Ministry, and Homeless Outreach. Sandra was also interviewed on radio shows such as Golden Life Living and WMAP Radio (World's Most Amazing People based out of New York), the Bill Martinez show, and a Fox Radio show called the Kim Kennedy Show.

She is a devoted mother of 2 sons (Tim & Gerald Ray), Gerald Ray the youngest, has gone on to be with the Lord due to a car accident. Through the death of her youngest son at the age of 16, a rocky marriage to an alcoholic and the abuse that came with that, and other overwhelming trials, she has drawn close to the loving arms of the Father. Experiencing God's unconditional love as He held her heart in His hands, has created a passion in her to help others grow in their understanding of and receive God's love and grow spiritually. She has the heart to help hurting women discover the princess in Christ that they truly are and overcome abuse. She teaches on topics to help you reach spiritual maturity, persevere through the hard times, and how to reach your destiny in Christ!